MW00531736

"If There's Anything I Can Do..."

"If There's Anything I Can Do..."

A Bookful of
Personal Experiences
and Good Ideas
on How to Help Those
Who Have Suffered Loss

Rebecca Bram Feldbaum

FELDHEIM PUBLISHERS
JERUSALEM · NEW YORK

ISBN 1-58330-577-7
First published 2003
Copyright © 2003 by Rebecca Bram Feldbaum

FELDHEIM PUBLISHERS
POB 35002 / Jerusalem, Israel
202 Airport Executive Park, Nanuet, NY 10954

www.feldheim.com

Printed in Israel

Rabbi CHAIM P. SCHEINBERG

Rosh Hayeshiva "TORAH ORE"

and Morah Hora'ah of Kiryat Mattersdorf

הרב חיים פינחס שיינברג

ראש ישיבת "תורה אור"

ומורה הוראה דקרית מטרסדורף

בס"ד-

בין המצרים תשס"ב

מיום שחרב בית המקדש אין יום שאין בו קללה As time goes on we hear more and more of misfortune striking with harsh severity. Many times the family or close friends are not properly prepared to cope with the tragedy.

Reb Dovid Feldbaum ז"ל was a dear talmid of our Yeshiva for many years. He was an outstanding example of a Ben Torah in his *midos* and character. His tragic passing had a profound impact on those who knew him. However, his dear widow suffered the most, as Chazal tell us, אין איש מת אלא לאשתו. In addition, she was left having to raise a family of small children while coping with a most difficult situation. As time passed, she realized that she was not alone. Hashem, the אבי יתומים ודיין אלמנות, looks after widows and orphans, caring for them in His very special way.

Mrs. Feldbaum תח' has written a memoir of her experiences in hope that it will help others who have to face tragedy and difficulties giving them the strength necessary to accept Hashem's hidden ways with love, growing in אמונה and בטחון.

My heartfelt brachos to Mrs. Feldbaum תח' that she should be able to continue raising her children in the true Torah spirit מתוך מנוחת הנפש והרחבת הדעת, and may her book be beneficial to others in helping them to understand the ways of Hashem.

ונזכה לראות בנחמת ציון וירושלים ולביאת גואל צדק במהרה בימינו.

Shearith Israel Congregation
קייק שארית ישראל
PARK HEIGHTS AND GLEN AVENUES
BALTIMORE, MARYLAND 21215

YAAKOV HOPFER, RABBI
466-3060 Study
358-8281 Residence

יעקב האפפער
באלטימאר, מד.

It is an honor and privilege for me to write words of recommendation on behalf of a remarkable woman, Mrs. Rebecca Feldbaum, and on behalf of her new book.

Mrs. Feldbaum has written a book about issues that require great sensitivity and understanding. There is no "one" way to deal with personal tragedy. Each person copes with pain and emotional turmoil in a way that is unique to him. Some people appreciate being spoken to constantly, while others need space and quiet. Most people desire companionship and support, however, they can be given in different ways. Some people will consider the words uttered by someone to be very sensitive, while others will consider these same words insensitive and damaging. As intelligent as a person might be, there is no way that he can feel and understand the emptiness, loneliness and pain of someone who has lost a spouse, unless he has personally lived through a similar situation. It is in that vein that I think Mrs. Feldbaum's book will be a great help and make a valuable contribution, as it will give the reader a keener insight into the heart and mind of the bereaved person.

Mrs. "Becca", as she is lovingly called in Baltimore, has known tragedy with the loss of her wonderful husband, Reb Dovid, z''l, who was a genuine gem. She has been an inspiration and guide to our community on how to live with adversity and make the best of it.

החתם בכבוד רב וברכ"ז
ויקרה ה/י000/ע

'עולם חסד יבנה'

Bikur Cholim of Baltimore

398 MT. WILSON LANE
PIKESVILLE, MARYLAND 21208
410-486-0322
FAX 410-484-8012

HONORARY MEMBERS
MR. MOSHE GOLDSTEIN
RABBI SHRAGA NEUBERGER
MRS. HANNAH STORCH

COMMITTEES
REBBITZEN CHANA WEINBERG
Coordinator

MRS. BERTHA NELKIN
MRS. GITTY KATZ
Hospital Visitation

MRS. MIRIAM SCHTAMF
Secretary

MRS. SANDY KATZ
Food Hospitality

MRS. ELAINE BERKOWITZ
Transportation

MRS. TOVA SALB
Visiting One on One

MS. DINA BLAUSTEIN
Pre-Natal Mitzvah Project

MRS. AMY DRABKIN
MRS. BRENDA STRUM
Giveras Yarden

REBBITZEN SARA KULEFSKY
Telephone

MRS. RACHEL BERNSTEIN
MRS. PAULY DREYFUSS
Tehillim Squad

MRS. JULIE MEISTER
All-Occasion Cards

MRS. DORIS GOLDSTEIN
MRS. BETH TENNENBAUM
Special Projects

(A Non-Profit Organization)

Feldheim Publishing Company

To Whom It May Concern:

I had the pleasure of working with Becca
Feldbaum and assisting on her manuscript.

This book is very much needed as a "How To",
not only for the general public but also for people
struggling with widowhood and other traumas in
their lives. The warmth, care and honest nature
of her words will surely be a support and
emotional help to anyone struggling with life's
issues. Her honest appraisal is an excellent road
map for people in all walks of life.

Most Sincerely,

Rebbetzin Chana Weinberg

Yeshiva Darchei Noam

of Monsey

4 Widman Court
Spring Valley, NY • 10977
845•352•7100
Fax•352•9593
Email•yhdarchei@aol.com

בס"ד

11 Kislev 5762
November 26, 2001

Having lost my father before my fourth birthday, I am especially touched by the wit and wisdom of Rebecca Feldbaum in her outstanding book.

Several years after the death of my father, my mother was fortunate to marry a devoted and caring man. Together, they rebuilt their lives, raised their children and led us to the *chuppa*.

During the years that she was alone, however, my mother's experience was, in many ways, strikingly similar to Mrs. Feldbaum's. She was often touched by and drew strength from the sensitivity and thoughtfulness of so many people. Sadly, she was also pained by the inadvertent comments of well-meaning people who offered their unsolicited advice on childrearing, family relations, and how she should be acting at any given time.

Many widows have commented to me that in addition to coming to terms with their tragedy and dealing with their loss, they are thrust in the uncomfortable position of living their lives in the public eye. They are too demanding of their children or spoiling them; walking around too cheerfully after the death of a loved one, or not bouncing back fast enough.

Mrs. Feldbaum has done a great service to the reading public by providing a window into the souls of our friends, neighbors and family members whose lives have been turned upside down by tragedy.

My *Hashem* grant her success in all her endeavors, and may she see continued *nachas* from her family.

With much admiration.

Rabbi Yakov Horowitz

DEDICATION
to my parents

This book is dedicated to my beloved parents,

Abraham Isaac ע"ה and **Lillian (Leba)** תבל"א

After my husband passed away, they sold their home in Little
Rock, Arkansas, and came to live with me and my children in
Baltimore, Maryland. Their presence was such a comfort in our
home, and they helped me out so much that I do not know what
I would have done without them.

My mother, who has the most genuinely giving nature of
any person I have ever known, was my primary example
throughout this book of how a person can truly be there for
others in their time of need. And, hopefully, everyone who reads
this book will come to really appreciate my father's favorite
saying whose words ring so loud and clear in these pages:
"If you have your health, then you have everything!"

May my mother continue to have much *nachas* from
her children and grandchildren.

IN MEMORY OF
לעילוי נשמת

Dovid ben Shmuel Ha-Kohen ז"ל
beloved husband and father

ת.נ.צ.ב.ה.

Contents

Chapter Eight

Appendices

Preface

In the Beginning...

At the age of twenty-eight, I married a wonderful man. At the age of thirty-seven I was widowed and left with four young children to raise.

Years earlier, a good friend, knowing how much I enjoyed writing, had given me a lined journal for a present. I had started writing in it in my "single days" and simply continued. After my nine-and-a-half years of marriage came to an end, my journal took on a much more poignant meaning for me. Whereas I had only written in it sporadically throughout the years, now I was seized with a passion to fill it with the torrent of all my private thoughts, feelings, and fears.

Since my children were so young when their father died, I also devoted a lot of effort to recording in my journal all of the happy times that we had shared together, so that I would remember to tell them these stories when they got older. I even began jotting down things people did for me or said to me that really helped me and my children during this hard period in our lives.

My family and friends were constantly asking me, "What can I say to comfort you? What can I do to help you and the kids?" They were all at a loss as to how to handle my situation, and, quite frankly, in many cases so was I. They began urging me to write a book telling people how they could help someone in my situation.

After flipping through my journal, I realized that I already had a lot of material to work with. I was very excited, since I had never entertained the idea before of writing a book and now I was contemplating writing one to make people more sensitive to what my children and I were going through.

As I got more serious, I bought a computer and began typing late into the night. I couldn't believe that the journal of stories I had originally intended to write just for my children was evolving into a solid, interesting manuscript! My journey to writing this book had now begun.

In the Middle...
When word got around that I was writing this type of book, widows from all over America and other countries began to contact me with suggestions about which subjects needed to be discussed. Speaking with them was a real learning experience for me. I heard about how life was for women with teenage children who had lost their husbands, and women with grown children living elsewhere who had lost their husbands, and women who were childless and had lost their husbands. They all had different obstacles to overcome. Yet I found their comments and insights extremely helpful and I began focusing intently on the many issues they had raised.

To my surprise, I was not only contacted by widows. I also spoke with people who had gone through other emotionally painful experiences, who wanted me to write about them, too. As my incredible "circle of friends" grew wider, I saw a clear relationship between their different stories and mine.

I decided not to limit myself to those who had gotten in touch with me through word of mouth. I interviewed people who I thought could make a worthwhile contribution to this book and I incorporated their ideas, as well.

For example, I spoke with widowers and divorced people about how they dealt with Shabbos and Yom Tov alone, what was involved in raising their children alone, and their feelings about looking for a new spouse. I also consulted with parents who had ill children about how one should conduct himself while visiting a sick individual in the hospital or at home and what helped their families the most during this stressful time. I spoke with adults who were teenagers when they lost a parent, in order to understand what their feelings were at this turbulent age. (I must add here that every person I spoke with who had lost a parent either while still a child or a teenager profusely thanked me for writing this book!) Then I consolidated all the information I had gathered and wrote about the topics they suggested or used their personal stories to illustrate the points I made.

Even though a majority of this book deals with what widows and their children go through and need, I have written it in such a way that it can also be used as a guide for how to be supportive of:

- ▶ Someone who has a sick relative or friend
- ▶ Someone who is handicapped or who has a family member who is
- ▶ Someone who is divorced, childless, or left as an *agunah* (a woman whose husband is missing or refuses to divorce his wife)
- ▶ Anyone who is suffering any other pain or loss

Whenever I discuss issues concerning a widow, the reader can certainly apply these same considerations to others. For example, in addition to helping a widow in the following ways, you can also help:

- ▶ A divorced or single person by inviting him/her to a Shabbos meal
- ▶ A handicapped person by including him/her in your family celebration
- ▶ A childless couple by remembering to send them *shalach manos* on Purim
- ▶ An elderly person who is living alone by occasionally visiting him/her

In this book, I have tried to show readers how they can act more compassionately towards others. To achieve this, however, it is very important to remember that each person is an individual. It is wrong to define a person by his category. People's needs are as individual as their feelings, and what is good for one person might very well offend another.

Years ago I read the book *Full Circle* by Gila Diamond (Feldheim Publishers). Her story of the trials, travails, and, in the end, triumph of a childless couple had a powerful impact on me. It made me much more empathetic towards my friends who didn't have any children. I hope that my book will have the same effect on readers who want to help others who are suffering for one reason or another.

And Now, at the End...
I will never forget the day when I watched the last page of my manuscript roll out of the printer. I had worked so hard, trying to find just the right words to express myself; I felt as though every single page was precious and in some way even a part of me. What an incredibly exhilarating feeling!

All I could think about was how much I hoped my children, my family, and friends would be proud of this book...and, of course, that everyone who read it would, as a result, know what to do and what to say to comfort someone in emotional distress.

Rebecca Bram Feldbaum

Chapter One:

How an Ending Was Transformed into a Beginning for Us

This part of the book contains a very personal account of the loss of our beloved husband and father, Dovid ben Shmuel HaKohen, beginning with his death. During Shivah, I started keeping a diary of my experiences, how I felt, and the lessons that I learned, thinking that one day I would turn it over to my children and hoping that it would mean as much to them as it has to me. Those notes, in fact, became the basis of this book.

What amazes me is how these stories portray the tremendous changes and growth that took place in my children and myself. Seeing in black and white how we each moved from such a terrible tragedy to live emotionally healthy, happy lives is a great source of comfort to me. With the unwavering help of family and friends, we have managed to rebuild ourselves into a strong and capable family unit.

Why am I making public here something that was so very private? To show you, the reader, what things are really like for a family who has lost a member they dearly loved. Hopefully, with this clear insight, you will become attuned to what others in this situation (or in a similarly painful situation) need from you. May Hashem bless you with enough awareness to act appropriately.

1

I had not slept for two days. The first night I was in the emergency room all night with Dovid. A good friend of mine, Sharon Rosen, who is a registered nurse, stayed with me the whole time, trying her best to make Dovid as comfortable as possible. I don't know what I would have done without her! The next night I was on a plane to Eretz Yisrael with my brother, Harris, and my two daughters — to bury my husband.

The last forty-eight hours have been such a whirlwind of activity. The tragic news; my friends packing for me and my daughters; parting from my two little boys who I was leaving with friends; the memorial service in Baltimore; flying to New York with my friend Dina and my girls; the emotional meeting with family and friends at the Newark Airport; then boarding the plane with Harris and my daughters for Israel.

We were allowed off the plane first, since the funeral was to begin in another hour and a half, and we were whisked through customs. My sister-in-law Dena Feldbaum and a very close friend, Miriam Freilich, met us at the airport. My brother and Dovid's brother, Avraham, Dena's husband, took Dovid to Yeshiva Torah Ore in Mattersdorf, where Dovid had studied and where the funeral was being held. All the women and girls went in another car with Dovid's best friend, Yisroel Chaim, to Dovid's Rebbe's house, Reb Dovid Krohn. Dena kept up a conversation with my daughters while I silently clung to Miriam's hand. Once in Mattersdorf, I decided to leave my daughters in the Krohn's apartment with their daughters until the funeral was over.

After I got the girls settled, I started to leave for the funeral. The Krohn's apartment was on an incline, overlooking the yeshiva, and I took a moment to look down at the crowd of all of our close friends. No one had seen me yet, but Dovid had already been brought there. Everyone was crying and praying... and my thoughts suddenly transported me back to another time and place.

It was my wedding day. Most of our close friends below had attended that glorious event. How happy everyone was then! Dovid was waiting for me under the *chuppah,* and I was walking down the aisle to him. Our life together would surely be a happy one — we were both certain about that. The question of how long that life together would be never even entered our minds.

Dovid had already reached the *chuppah* and everyone was waiting for me to come... as they were all waiting for me now. And, in a spiritual way, so was Dovid. I gazed out at my friends who had come from all over Israel to be with me. But this time they were not waiting to share with me the happiest day of my life — but the saddest.

Holding tightly again to Miriam's hand, I took a deep breath and slowly began walking down to my husband's funeral.

*   *   *

"*HaMakom yenacheim osach b'toch she'ar avelei Tzion vi'Yerushalayim* — May Hashem console you among the other mourners of Zion and Jerusalem."

I could not believe it. The first time someone said those words to me the reality of the whole situation crashed down upon me. I was a thirty-seven-year-old widow with four small children, ages two, four, six, and seven.

Sitting on a low stool surrounded by the comforting, protective love of family and friends, my tears flowed freely. I was sitting *Shivah* for the wonderful husband I had waited twenty-eight years to find. Now, only nine-and-a-half years later, I was mourning him in the traditional Jewish manner prescribed by our Jewish Sages.

Throughout the week, friends I had not seen or heard from in years came to the house. I felt such mixed emotions — happiness at seeing long-lost acquaintances and sadness when

thinking about the circumstances that had brought us together once again.

This was the first time I had ever been in mourning, and I
had no clear idea of what I was supposed to do. So I tried to
listen hard to what people said to comfort me. Many of my
visitors fell into the following categories:

▶ **People who could not speak.** They were so pained by
my loss that no words could pass through their lips. The
wringing of their hands, the gentle tapping of their shoes on
the floor, the way their heads were bowed, and their mourn-
ful eyes told me volumes without having to hear them utter
a single word.

▶ **People who knew my husband at different stages of
his life and told me stories about him.** I took every word of
theirs to heart and treasured the memories they shared with
me. I heard a lot of things I never knew about Dovid before,
and each new tale was a true source of comfort for me.

▶ **People who came to tell me how proud they were of
me!** They had heard that Dovid and I had gone through such
an incredibly difficult situation together and that we had remained strong in our religious convictions. They also told me
that they knew we had done everything we possibly could to
get Dovid the best treatment, while taking care of our four
children at the same time. How I needed to hear their words!

▶ **People who reminisced about the happy times they
had seen my husband and I share.** How wonderful to relive
happy memories in spite of my intense feelings of loss. And
even though it hurt me to realize that those good times together were over, I also felt very grateful that we had had
them.

▶ **People who totally understood my feelings of pain
and loss and who came to cheer me up with their own good
news.** Two friends who had suffered from childlessness for

years came to tell me that they now each had been blessed with a child. Two other friends who were divorced came to tell me about their happy remarriages! One friend, whose husband had been critically ill, told me about the miracle of his complete recovery!

"Hashem, Hashem!" I cried out silently. "Thank You for sending me these wonderful friends." How I needed to hear their joyous stories while sitting in my cave of gloom.

Eventually, I felt a small ray of light (my happiness for them) begin to penetrate and the heavy weight pressing on my heart lifted a bit. It was so good to be reminded that even though I was presently suffering, there still was some happiness out there, maybe even for me one day.

Although my body was sitting still, my thoughts were racing. I wanted to draw out everyone's thoughts and stories about Dovid and completely envelop myself in them. Each story was like a lifeline for me, keeping alive my connection to Dovid and preventing me from drowning in my overwhelming sorrow.

Behind my head, on the bookshelf above my seat, was a picture taken three months earlier of Dovid and me at a friend's son's Bar Mitzvah. Dovid was very thin then and people who saw it were shocked. Yet it gave me great comfort to know he was still behind me, and in my heart and thoughts he always would be.

I learned a lot — about other people and about myself — during the week of *Shivah*. Some things made me feel good and other things were pretty hard to deal with. But with *siyyata di'Shemaya* — God's help — I made it through the seven days of mourning.

When I stood up from *Shivah* and walked through my front door for the first time on that October morning in Jerusalem, I headed straight for the Kotel. I knew I had become a different person — stronger and more sensitive to others, no longer a wife, but much more a mother and, in a sense, a father, too.

*   *   *

It was Friday night and my sister-in-law Dena and I had just lit Shabbos candles. The house was very lively with her boys jumping all over the place. I needed the distraction badly. It was my first Shabbos without Dovid.

We went out on her balcony, which overlooked the Ramot neighborhood in Jerusalem. Of course, my tears could not help but fall. I was so glad that my girls were absorbed in the antics of their cousins and not looking at me.

My brother-in-law Avraham came home and everyone joined him as he began singing "*Shalom Aleichem.*" At once I was jolted out of my sorrow. I was hearing my husband's voice — the Southern twang, slightly off-tune, but filled with warmth and feeling for the sanctity of Shabbos. I looked at my daughters and noticed that my older one was staring at her uncle. I worried how this would affect her.

It was the same with *Kiddush* and the Shabbos *zemiros* that we sang. After one particularly long song, my daughter said, "Uncle Avraham, you have such a beautiful voice!"

My sister-in-law Dena and I looked at each other and burst out laughing! She turned to her husband and said, "You should be thrilled. In all the years we've been married, no one's ever complimented you on your singing ability!"

My daughter, not understanding what was behind our laughter said, "But he does have a beautiful voice. He sounds just like my Tatti!"

*   *   *

I had been waiting to take this bus ride for two-and-a-half years. Ever since Dovid's illness was diagnosed, I had yearned to go to the Kotel. I would close my eyes while I was praying for his recovery and imagine over and over again that I was touching those sacred stones. And now, I was on my way.

When I was living in Yerushalayim as a single young woman, I tried to go to the Kotel weekly. As a wife, I went once a month. And as a mother, well... whenever I could, until we returned to America.

I boarded a bus in the Har Nof neighborhood with my two daughters for a l-o-n-g glorious ride to the Kotel. I had just gotten up from *Shivah* that morning and this was our first "outing." I breathlessly took in the sights that I had missed so much! Excitedly, I pointed out to my girls the neighborhoods of Givat Shaul, Kiryat Mattersdorf, Ezras Torah, etc. and they strained their necks to look at everything I was showing them.

In between my narrations, my six-year-old kept up an animated chatter about her father that went like this, "Tatti died. That's why we're here. If Tatti hadn't died, we'd be in school. But he died. So we're in Eretz Yisrael. Because, Tatti died." It didn't upset me to hear what she was saying, because I realized she was just trying to sort things out.

A Chassid who was sitting near us was engrossed in his *Sefer Tehillim*. Right before he got off the bus, he blessed my children and me. I guess even though he was busy reciting Psalms, he couldn't avoid hearing my child's recitation of why we were there. (I convinced myself that he was Eliyahu *HaNavi*, but later found out that he was really a good friend of my brother-in-law!)

At last we arrived. I just could not wait to walk the last few yards to get to the Kotel and pray. As we were approaching, I was stopped and asked to give *tzedakah*. I gave my girls some coins and they dispensed them to whoever asked.

And then it happened. A woman in old clothes, who wanted *tzedakah* too, came over and began tugging on my sleeve. As she pulled at me she said, "*Geveret, bevakashah. Ani almanah* — Missus, please. I am a widow."

I will never forget that moment. Everything around me started to spin. I felt like I couldn't breathe. The woman kept saying it over and over again, louder and louder, "*Ani almanah! Ani almanah!*" as though I didn't understand.

I wanted to scream back at her, "*GAM ANI! GAM ANI ALMANAH!* — ME TOO! I'M ALSO A WIDOW!"

My daughters saw the pained look on my face and called out "Mommy!" That broke through my anxiety and returned me to myself. I gave the woman some coins, took my daughters' hands, and resumed walking.

We stopped to wash at a basin of water before entering the prayer area. How I wanted to tell my daughters that this was where their Tatti and I officially got engaged, but the words wouldn't come. I took them close to the Kotel and they began to recite the prayers that they knew.

I could not bring myself to open a *Siddur* or *Tehillim*. This was the Kotel, where I had poured out my fervent prayers to get married. Yes, I had done that. But the man that I had prayed for was no longer here with me. Dovid. My beloved Dovid.

I tried hard not to let the girls see how distressed I was. But the woman's words kept reverberating in my ears, "*Ani almanah! Ani almanah!*" The surrounding buildings, the beautiful view, the Kotel itself had not changed much since I'd left Israel several years ago. But I, Rebecca Bram Feldbaum, had changed — I was now an *almanah*.

Note: I did manage to visit the Kotel a few more times before I went back to America. On those occasions, I was able to pour out my feelings to Hashem about becoming a widow. And even with all of my fears, I always felt an inner calm whenever I touched the Kotel and prayed.

I did not understand, of course, why Hashem had taken Dovid out of this world at such a young age, leaving behind his young widow and children. But I knew I had to go on for the children's sake. And so, I prayed to Him to give me the strength to get through this tremendous *nisayon*, this great test in my life.

* * *

We arrived back in Baltimore and I was about to enter my house for the first time after burying my husband. I sent my daughters across the street to a friend's house so I could have a few moments alone. My close friend, Miriam Robbins, had picked us up from the airport and was helping me bring our luggage to the front porch. We looked at each other and she said, "Ready?"

I gingerly replied, "As ready as I'll ever be."

We opened the door and stepped inside. As I stood in the middle of the living room, I thought, Now I know what the expression "'heavy heart" really means.

I closed my eyes as the tears silently coursed down my face. Miriam gave me a hug and wisely did not speak. She had been left a widow many years before and she knew I needed time to gather my thoughts.

On the day Dovid died, when we left for the airport, the house looked like it had been hit by a hurricane. Friends piled into the house to pack for me. Suitcases were all over the beds and clothes were strewn everywhere! One friend would pack what she thought we needed and then another friend would unpack what the first one had packed and put in different things she thought we would need. Plus, our sad news had traveled fast and the phone was constantly ringing. The noise and the mess were unbelievable.

Now, the oppressive silence pierced me to the bone. Slowly, I surveyed my home. It was now absolutely spotless! I walked from room to room. Everything, everywhere was immaculate. The refrigerator was filled with milk, fruit, vegetables, cheese… and a casserole that someone had brought over for dinner. There was a note taped to the refrigerator door welcoming us back and telling me that we would be receiving suppers for a month!

I went upstairs and smiled when I saw the bathroom. New bright blue curtains were on the windows. A brand new set consisting of a bathroom rug and toilet seat cover, as well as new towels, adorned the room.

Entering the master bedroom was the hardest. The beds were neatly made up and the bed quilts looked like they had been washed as well. "Our" closet was now "my" closet. Slowly I opened it. My clothes hung inside by themselves looking, I thought, very lonely.

My dresser was the same, but Dovid's was now completely empty. I opened each drawer and felt grateful to my friends who, after asking my permission, had cleaned them out for me.

I had asked them to save Dovid's ties, suspenders, caps, Shabbos hat, lunch box, and briefcase for the boys to play with. They had left me a neatly labeled box containing these items in the back of the closet. I couldn't get over how much my friends had done while I was gone.

I sat down on my bed and rested for a minute. My heart was not racing anymore. Then, after awhile I heard a familiar voice calling, "Becca, please come down here. There are some children who would like to see you."

I hurried down the stairs to my little boys and got a great big hug and kiss from my four-year-old son. My youngest child, age two, hung back. He was holding the hand of the dear, close friend whom he had stayed with these past three weeks. I gently ruffled his hair and said, "Michoel, do you know who I am?" He smiled and replied, "I know you! You are Mommy!" Then he gave me a big hug.

Yes, Mommy was back.

Note: Please do not ever clean out the deceased's clothing and belongings unless you are specifically asked to do so. Everyone experiences grief differently, and some family members might feel great comfort doing this themselves.

*   *   *

It was my first Shabbos back in the United States. I had already spent three Sabbaths without my husband, so I thought that I was getting used to it. Friday night I wanted just the five of us to be together.

Preparing for that Shabbos was very hard. I kept wondering how I would survive it without Dovid, as well as the many more that were to come. Shabbos was supposed to be a day of peace, yet my mind was in an upheaval over all that had happened to our — my — family. How would I ever again be able to relax on this day?

I tried to keep my spirits up by playing music (since the thirty-day *Sheloshim* period a wife is supposed to mourn for her husband was already over for me). Friends brought over a delicious Shabbos meal so I didn't have much to prepare. Yet the sadness was so pervasive, you could have cut it with a knife. Alone, alone, alone. Just like the twenty-eight years of Sabbaths that had passed until I got married. But this time I was alone with four special little ones to take care of. What a responsibility!

I lit Shabbos candles and felt a calm descend upon me. Then came a knock at the door. It was Rabbi Nosson Freedman from across the street, coming to take my eldest son to shul. Moshe gladly reached for Rabbi Freedman's hand and away they went. But it was very difficult for me — my son no longer had a father to take him to shul.

I tried unsuccessfully to push away all of the negative thoughts that were invading my mind. Who would learn with Moshe? Who would show him how to put on tefillin when he was older? And, well, who would teach him how to throw a curve ball?

Later, a few of my friends came over to wish me a "Good Shabbos." My children played happily with their children. The words were unspoken, but it was obvious who was on all of our minds.

Moshe returned from shul and all of my friends left except for one, Dina. She had flown with the girls and me to New York, where we caught our connecting flight to Eretz Yisrael. The kids adore her and affectionately call her Tante D. She was going to be eating somewhere else a little later, so she decided to stay with me until I recited *Kiddush* and said the *HaMotzi* blessing over bread.

I sat in my husband's place at the head of the table. We sang "*Shalom Aleichem*" and then I told the children to line up so I could bless them like their father always did. I could barely get the words out because my voice and hands were trembling so much.

I then turned to Dina and pleaded with her to eat with us tonight. She graciously went with one of my children to tell the family she was invited to eat with that she would be eating with us instead. That gave me a little time to get my emotions in place before I made *Kiddush*.

The kids thought that all of this was quite amusing: Mommy sitting in Tatti's place, Mommy giving them a blessing, and making *Kiddush* and then *HaMotzi* over the bread.

Dina was wonderful — making conversation with the kids and helping me in the kitchen and then reading to the kids and helping me put them to bed. I couldn't even thank her properly. I was so emotional about everything that I could hardly speak. I fell into a fitful sleep as soon as she left.

The next morning I felt a little more prepared to face the day. We were invited to our good friends, Judy and Adean Zapinsky, for Shabbos lunch and off we went.

As we were walking to the Zapinskys, people started coming out of shul. I noticed the uncomfortable looks and stares directed at my family. No one seemed to know how to greet us or what to say. Fortunately, one friend of mine, Sury Goldman, hurried over to us as soon as she saw us to wish us a "Good Shabbos." That meant the world to me! It also broke the ice and others called out greetings, too.

Once we arrived, I breathed a sigh of relief. That was the longest five blocks I had ever walked!

I spent the meal getting used to handling all of my children in public alone. *Baruch Hashem,* they behaved nicely.

Around the middle of the meal, my oldest son suddenly said he didn't feel well. I asked him what was wrong and he told me that his stomach itched. I pulled up his shirt to have a look and sure enough, he was covered with chicken pox!

I looked Heavenward and said, "Thank you, Hashem, for thinking I am capable of handling so many things right now!" Then Judy and I burst out laughing! (I was relieved to hear that she was still laughing about two weeks later when her kids broke out with the chicken pox, too!)

So much for my hopes of an uneventful first Shabbos back in the States!

*   *   *

It should have been just an ordinary day, but my situation was not so ordinary anymore and I was just going to have to realize that. The kids were in school and I was supposed to go to the dermatologist, then to the bank to deposit some checks, and then off to the grocery store. What could be so bad?

I arrived at the dermatologist's office and signed in. My eczema was acting up from all the stress I was feeling. I hadn't been to his office in over a year, since I had unfortunately been busy with other things, so I had to fill out a new form for insurance purposes. No big deal.

I started filling it out and then came to the line where I had to circle one of the following regarding my marital status: S (single)/M (married)/D (divorced)/W (widowed).

I squeezed the pen hard and silently screamed, "No, no, no! I don't want to circle W! I don't want to be in this category! I want to circle M! I want my husband back! I want to be married!" I filled out the rest of the questionnaire and at the last moment circled W.

I gave the receptionist the form and headed back to my seat. "Just hold it in, Becca!" I kept telling myself. "For heaven's sake, don't cry in the doctor's office!"

My name was called and I went into one of the examination rooms. I tried to calm myself down, but all I could do was to stare unhappily out of the second floor window.

My dermatologist finally entered the room. He is a very pleasant man, always with a warm smile and a friendly greeting. "How are you doing?" he asked me. "I haven't seen you for a long time."

What could I say? Well, I blurted it all out — my husband had recently died; my eczema was driving me crazy because of all the pressures of being a single parent; I was under a lot of stress; and I had just circled W for the first time. Oh, yes, I even told him that! He was extremely sympathetic and very kind.

Afterwards, I went to the bank. "Becca, you will be okay. You will be okay," I kept repeating to myself. I needed to deposit some checks and then I remembered what they were — my first Social Security checks, the payments that spouses and children collect when a spouse/parent passes away. As I gave them to the teller, tears rolled down my cheeks. I didn't want to deposit these! This was not what I wanted to live on! I wanted to be depositing my husband's salary!

When the teller asked me if everything was all right, I replied, "This is the first time I'm depositing Social Security checks. I just lost my husband."

He was a young man, but I will never forget the sympathetic look on his face. He said, "Mrs. Feldbaum, if there is anything this bank can do for you, please let us know!" I thanked him, finished the transaction, and walked out.

Once safely inside my car, I began sobbing. I felt like I couldn't do ANYTHING without being constantly reminded of my new status. I knew the wound was still too fresh and the pain too raw.

I skipped the visit to the store that day and took some time for myself — I went for a walk, ate lunch leisurely, and read a magazine. I also kept repeating the following words to myself, "Things will get better. I just need to take one day at a time. One day at a time!"

*   *   *

We were sitting around the dinner table one evening when one of my kids mentioned that she had learned a new number game. You have to choose a number between one and twenty and then everyone has to guess what it is. Of course everyone wanted to play, so we went around the table taking turns.

When it was my two-year-old son's turn to choose, he pointed his finger at each of us, letting us know when it was our turn to guess. As it turned out, none of us guessed the right number, so he pointed his finger straight up towards the ceiling and said, "Tatti, what is the number?" My other children looked at me and I froze.

Then I just covered my mouth with my hand and said in a deep, booming voice, "Three."

"Wrong!" my son announced, and pointed to his brother to pick another number. My kids squealed with laughter.

Every time a child took a turn, he would also point up to the ceiling and say, "It's Tatti's turn!" and I would call out a number in as masculine a voice as I could muster! They all loved it.

How did I feel?, you might ask. WONDERFUL, WONDERFUL, WONDERFUL! Even though Dovid was no longer physically with us, the kids still thought of him as part of our family unit. One simple little game let me know that he was still with us. It meant a lot to me.

*   *   *

I got my first "whammie" a month after we returned from Israel. I'm talking about a migraine headache so intense that I could hardly bear it.

I was frightened and didn't know what to do because the children would be coming home from school and I wasn't well enough to take care of them. I called up a friend for help and she mobilized some of my other friends to take care of the kids through bedtime. One of their daughters even slept on our living room couch that night, to handle any night duty that might be needed.

I thought that the migraine was just an isolated incident, but the next week the same thing happened. After that second horrible day, I made an appointment with my doctor. A battery of tests and a full physical exam produced a diagnosis of pure and simple stress! She gave me a prescription for a stronger pain reliever, and it helped ease the symptoms whenever I got a "whammie."

I told some of my single-mother friends about it and they said that they had suffered from similar problems during their first year of parenting alone. Some had experienced headaches, some had broken out in terrible skin rashes, some had developed stomach problems or heartburn, while others had suffered from insomnia. Even though I felt bad about their troubles, I was greatly relieved to learn that what I was experiencing was normal.

*   *   *

The sound downstairs startled me. The kids were asleep and I distinctly heard something or someone rattling my front door. My first instinct was to call 911, but I waited a minute to be sure. Silence.

With my cordless phone in hand, I cautiously crept down the stairs. I still heard nothing and the front door was closed all the way. Thankfully the chain was still on. When I reached the bottom step, I spotted the source of the sound: an envelope was lying on the floor next to the mail slot.

I picked it up and saw that it was addressed to me. Tearing it open, I found a note inside that said, "For you, dear Rebecca. To help you out with whatever you need." Enclosed were two hundred-dollar bills.

Over the next few months, more envelopes were dropped in my mail slot with varying amounts of money. It was hard for me be the recipient of so much goodwill, but I had no way of returning the money, since none of them bore a return address.

Those envelopes were not just filled with money, but also with care, love, and... hope. And, they were greatly appreciated.

*   *   *

Every Monday night, I attend a weekly *shiur* on the weekly Torah portion given by a very special Rav in our community, Rabbi Simcha Shafran. Even when Dovid was sick, I tried to go so that I could have some semblance of a "normal" life.

After Dovid passed away, I wasn't able to face going for a few months. Finally, with the encouragement of friends, I went back. The group greeted me warmly. I was glad to be back and involved in something that I really enjoyed. Surprisingly enough, I was even able to concentrate on the topic and not feel jittery or distracted, as the case had been with other things I'd tried to do these past few months.

After the lecture a friend drove me home and picked up her daughter, who was babysitting for my kids. As I closed the door behind me, I was greeted by a deafening silence that found its way inside me. No matter how ill Dovid had been those last few months, he had always stayed up to greet me when I came home and ask me what I had learned. There was no one asking now.

I felt engulfed in sadness. "Dovid, Dovid!" I cried out silently. "Don't you want to know what I learned tonight? You were always very proud of me that I kept up my learning. I so much want to tell you about it now. Who can I talk to? Who will be waiting for me when I come home from the *shiur* next week? What am I going to do?"

I folded my arms and held myself tightly as I trudged up the stairs to the bedrooms. I could not believe the force of what had come over me. I went to each of my children and gave them a kiss. I listened to them breathe. I smelled their sweet smells. It was after 10:00 P.M. and I didn't know what to do. I was beside myself with loneliness.

Then the telephone rang. It was a friend. "It was so nice to see you at the *shiur* tonight, Becca," she said. "I know it must have been hard for you, but everyone was glad that you came."

Saying those words was like throwing me a life preserver. I needed to hear that someone still cared, even though I was not hearing it from the person that I missed the most.

She was a close friend, and so I told her how much her phone call meant to me and what emotions I was feeling then. She immediately wanted to come over — and her husband told her to — but I insisted that she stay home. I had just needed a caring adult voice to pierce the crushing solitude enveloping me at that moment. And her thoughtful words had done the trick. Reassuring her that I had really only needed to tell her what was in my heart, I got off the line — with a promise that I would call her anytime during the night if I felt that overwhelming sadness again.

I got ready for bed. I cried in the shower. I kissed the kids again. I had that scoop of ice cream that I had resisted a few hours earlier. And, with all emotion drained from me, I went peacefully to sleep.

Thank you, Hashem, for giving me such wonderful friends.

*   *   *

We walk slowly up the block, arm in arm — I, the new, young widow, and she, the widow of many, many years. She has graced our Shabbos table countless times, and to keep our friendship strong, she visits on Shabbos afternoons to see how we are. She is worried about me with my new responsibilities and I worry about her and her health.

Despite her protests, I walk her up the street to her home. Unfortunately, after four months I know the feeling of walking alone, without having anyone to worry about my safety or well-being. Once we are in front of her house, she insists on watching me walk back home. It is cold and I do not want her to get chilled, so I hurry. I pass other people's houses and hear happy voices shouting to one another. Families! Whole units!

I turn to wave and get a wave in return. She climbs the steps to her too-silent house and the beginning of another quiet night. I climb the steps, knowing the noise that awaits me. But both our homes are filled with loneliness, and we try to reach out to one another to make it a little easier to bear.

*   *   *

The kids excitedly asked me what we were going to do for Dovid's 41st birthday — the first one since he passed away. Their question totally floored me. A birthday party for a father who died? Such a thing had never even entered my mind! But, they were so gung-ho about celebrating it that I went along with them.

The evening of Dovid's birthday, I ordered in pizza. I just couldn't bear the idea of going out and hearing my kids publicly announce what we were celebrating. And so, we had a pizza and ice cream party. I must admit it turned out to be a wonderful idea. We talked about what the children remembered about their Tatti and looked at picture albums of him with them. It brought back very good memories for all of us.

After that, we made this into a family tradition. Friends have suggested to me that this is a morbid practice, but I see it as a very original and upbeat way for them to honor the memory of their father.

*   *   *

One night, as I was putting my younger daughter Chaya Gittel to bed, she frantically began to search for something. She told me that she needed to find an envelope, and fortunately, she found it near her pillow. She excitedly showed me why it was so important to her.

The envelope was addressed to "Tatti Feldbaum." Inside was a note to her father telling him how much she loved and missed him. Also included were a picture she had colored, some money (twenty cents), and a sticker.

"Mommy, when will Tatti come down from *Shamayim* and take this envelope? I left it here a few days ago for him and he hasn't picked it up." I told her I didn't know.

I went downstairs, thinking that I did not want to take the envelope away while she was sleeping, because I did not want her to get the impression that her Tatti could just come down from Heaven and zoom into her room at night. I decided to call Devorah Klein, the grief therapist who was working with the girls, to hear what she had to say about this.

She agreed that I could not let her think that her Tatti could come whenever she wanted him. We did not want to give her an unrealistic understanding of death. We decided to tell her to put the envelope in her *Siddur* and when she prayed she could have her Tatti in mind and the thoughts of how much she missed and loved him would reach him in *Shamayim*.

I went upstairs to tell Chaya Gittel, but she was fast asleep. Her hand was under her pillow, holding the envelope. I brushed back her hair and kissed her forehead.

Tomorrow I would tell her. For now, I would leave it close to her head — and her heart.

Note: Last year my older son was very proud of a grade he had gotten and he wanted to know if Tatti was aware of how well he had done.

"Mommy! I have a great idea," he said. "Why don't we try dialing 1-800-SHAMAYIM and see if we can reach Tatti that way?"

A few weeks ago my younger son (now age 8) was telling me how he wished Tatti could join us for Purim. He wanted to know if Tatti had an e-mail address where we could reach him!

All of my children wanted to make some form of contact with their father, be it through messages under a pillow, or the phone company, or the computer! I have given each one of them the same sound advice Devorah gave me six years ago — that when they pray they can send a special message to their Tatti and he will receive it. (Believe me, I would love it if 1-800-SHAMAYIM worked and I could get some answers to a few of my questions!)

*   *   *

We went to my brother's home for the first Sukkos, Shemini Atzeres and Simchas Torah Festivals after Dovid died.
The kids had a great time with their cousins for the whole
week, and on the night of Simchas Torah, we all went to shul
with my brother. The synagogue was packed with happy
adults and enthusiastic children. With each round of dancing
with the Torah, the atmosphere seemed to take on a more
vibrant intensity.

My brother was valiantly trying to dance both with my
sons and his younger children. During one particularly lively
dance (where the children had to be held high or trampled),
it was my nephew's turn to be held by his father. My older
son was running around with his other cousins, but my
younger son wanted to dance in the men's circle and I could
not persuade him to stay with me.

Not knowing what to do, he simply stood outside the circle and held up his hands. He wasn't crying or yelling in order to be noticed; he just quietly stood there with his hands
stretched above his head — looking at all the men and waiting for someone to pick him up.

I felt my heart break, seeing him there with his hands
outstretched — and his Tatti not around to pick him up. After a few minutes my brother noticed him and motioned for
him to come and join in the circle, but just then, someone
dancing beside my brother asked him who this young child
was. My brother told him the situation and this man just
swooped my son up into his arms and danced with him for
the rest of the evening.

I fled to the women's bathroom and sobbed into my fists
for a long, long time. Even though, thank God, someone had
been kind to my son, it still hurt me so much that Dovid was
not there to dance with him.

In my mind's eye I can still see young Michoel Simcha
with his hands stretched upwards, standing outside that

circle of men. It is an image that I will certainly never, ever forget.

*   *   *

My daughter, Raizel, went to a sleep-over party at the home of her new friend Batya. (Batya's family had just moved to Baltimore a few months before.) The next day, when the party was over and it was time to go home, Uncle Avi (Raizel's best friend's father) came to the front door and told Batya's sister, "I'm here to pick up Raizel and Esti." She ran downstairs to the roomful of girls and loudly announced to everyone, "Raizel, your Tatti is here to pick up you and Esti."

"Mommy," Raizel told me, "everyone was silent. They just stared at me. They didn't know what to say. Even I didn't know what to say. Finally, my friend Ayala said, 'Well, I don't think it could be Raizel's Tatti!' I was so happy that she broke the tension! All of us started to laugh, and Esti and I left."

*   *   *

I went out to dinner one evening with a friend and her husband. After we were seated, the waiter came over and inquired, "And when will your husband be arriving?" After a moment of silence, I replied, "It's just the three of us this evening."

*   *   *

"Mommy, Mommy, hurry and come!" I heard my name being urgently called and I rushed down the stairs. The kids were huddled in front of the open closet and pointing at something.

I pushed my way to the front and saw "it" — a big, black bug. Oh, yuck!

I ordered one of my kids to go upstairs and get my tennis shoe. He returned in record time and the bug was dispensed with. Another child ran to get a paper towel and "it" was thrown into the garbage. Mommy Feldbaum — exterminator. My kids were looking at me as their big, brave mother. Little did they know that I couldn't wait to get into a shower and wash off the whole buggy incident.

I had become their main protector in this world. The kids were always running to me to save them: from a bee in the backyard, a down-the-street bully, a neighbor's loose dog, and even one night, from a particularly noisy rainstorm.

It wasn't that I never killed a bug when Dovid was alive or calmed them down during a thunderstorm when he was away on business, but now I HAD to be the brave one all of the time — and I really didn't want to. I had to maintain this image for my children; they were dependent on me for their safety and well-being.

I want my children to feel as secure as possible in their one-parent home, and so, I squash yucky bugs and get their bikes back from bullies and swat away bees. Yet, I must admit, when they cuddle up with me under the covers at night during a thunderstorm, I do not mind at all.

*   *   *

My tenth wedding anniversary was fast approaching. Nine-and-a-half years of a wonderful relationship. Did one celebrate a wedding anniversary by oneself? Just what was I supposed to do? I felt I had to do SOMETHING. After all, Dovid would have wanted our wedding date to be remembered as a joyous occasion and not one of sadness.

As I reviewed my memories of the past nine years, I knew that I had to make it a special occasion for me. So, I decided to buy myself something. But I couldn't think of anything I really needed or wanted. And then the idea struck me. What better way to celebrate our anniversary than to remember what our nine years together had produced — four wonderful children!

One morning I got the kids up and bathed, their hair combed to near perfection and wearing their matching Shabbos outfits, and we headed for the Sears Portrait Studios. I took my good friend Dina (who my kids affectionately call Tante D) along with me, because I was sure she would get them to smile.

When our turn came, the girls stood up straight and tall, while the boys sat quietly with hands folded in their laps. Getting them all to smile nicely was a bit of a challenge, but they finally did and we were done.

I waited impatiently for weeks to get the pictures. Dina came with me to pick them up and I opened the large envelope with trepidation. We were both stunned at the beautiful photos: all smiles, everyone's eyes open, every hair in place...

And so, on the night of my anniversary, after putting my children to bed, I went downstairs, sat in the rocking chair and clutched the framed 8"x10" Sears picture of the children to my chest. I must have rocked for over an hour, but I was determined not to cry. Tonight I was celebrating the beautiful legacy my husband had left in this world. And I prayed that our children would always have those smiles on their faces.

*   *   *

It was a beautiful Shabbos day and I had been invited to attend a Bar Mitzvah in the synagogue around the corner. At the end of the service, while the congregation was singing one of the final hymns, my son stood on the chair next to me and put his small hand in mine. He looked down through the *mechitzah* separating the men's women's sections, at the men below and then whispered in my ear, "Mommy, which one is my Tatti?"

I thought I hadn't heard him right and asked him to repeat the question. "My Tatti!" he said. "Down there. Which one is my Tatti?"

I'll tell you what my first reaction was. I gazed down at the sea of black hats and I wanted to reach down and whisk one of the men up to my son and say, "Here he is! Here's your Tatti!" With so many men down there, surely one wouldn't be missed?

But with a catch in my throat I whispered back to him, "Now you tell me, where is your Tatti?" He gave me one of his toothy grins and shyly pointed Heavenward.

"That's right, sweetie," I said. "Even though we can't see him, you do have a Tatti. And he loves you very much and is very proud of you." That seemed to satisfy him — for now.

*   *   *

It was just a normal day, but I was utterly exhausted. I silently thanked Hashem for giving me the strength that day to: drive the car pool, make breakfast, lunch, and supper, wash and dry two loads of laundry and put it away, fill the car with gas, go to the supermarket, straighten up the house, take the kids to the library after supper — I was sure there was more, but I couldn't even remember.

After putting the children to bed, hoping they would fall asleep right away, I could hear them giggling and sneaking in and out of bed. It seems that whenever I am the most worn out, they are the most rambunctious.

I felt so sorry for myself at that moment. How I wished that I had my husband back to help me in the evenings. I suddenly felt that I just couldn't deal with quieting the boys down and cleaning up the kitchen after dinner.

I dragged myself over to the couch to rest a little and to regain my strength. I'll just take a few minutes off, I told myself, trying to calm down.

I must have dozed off, for I suddenly felt someone on the couch next to me. It was my daughter, who was giving me one of her great back massages! I could feel my tension start to dissolve.

Then I felt someone gently taking off my shoes. I peeked from the corner of one of my closed eyes and saw my youngest child at work. He had brought a blanket with him and tried to cover me with it. And then, despite the loudly whispered protests of his siblings, he lifted my head, put another pillow under it, and "softly" dropped my head back down! Then everyone "tip-toed" out of the room.

I heard the boys quiet down, so I assumed that the girls were reading them books. When I woke up (an hour later!), a beautiful stillness had descended on the house. I went to check on the children, who were all fast asleep. And, lo and behold, when I went into my kitchen, it was all cleaned up! Suddenly, I felt unbelievably loved and cared for.

Being a single parent definitely has its ups and downs, but it's nights like this one that show me how well we all take care of each other.

*   *   *

It was P.T.A. night at my girls' school. I was dashing back and forth from classroom to classroom, since I had to speak with both daughters' English, Hebrew, and reading group teachers. I was having a good time chatting with my friends in the hallways, too.

"Mrs. Feldbaum," one of their teachers said, "I just have to tell you a story about something that happened in my classroom a few weeks ago. I handed out papers to the class and told the girls to take one home and have their mother sign it. One of my students raised her hand and informed me that she didn't have a mother. So then I said they should have their father sign it. Then your daughter raised her hand and said she didn't have a father! So I said they could have any parent sign it. That made me realize that I have to be very careful how I phrase things."

I thanked the teacher for telling me, because this particular daughter had felt a little embarrassed that her Tatti had died, since it made her different from her friends in a major way. To me, it showed progress that she could make such a statement in public.

As I walked back out into the hallway, preparing to go home, I saw an acquaintance coming towards me, a woman whom I knew a little, but who had avoided me like the plague since my husband died. She literally would change aisles in the supermarket if she saw me approaching.

Right then and there, I decided that if my daughter could get over feeling uncomfortable about what had happened to her father, then this acquaintance could too. I made a beeline for her and saw a look of panic cross her face. Greeting her warmly, I asked about her daughter, who was a classmate of my daughter. We spoke for maybe thirty seconds, but it was enough to break the tension between us since Dovid had died.

I left the school filled with a new optimism. My children and I might have a home situation that was different from others, but we would teach the world how to deal with us anyway... as we slowly learned ourselves.

*   *   *

For a year — and in some cases for years — after Dovid died, I could not bring myself to make certain foods that he had liked... or to even buy them. To this day there is one particular cereal that he really enjoyed that I still think would be just too painful for me to see in my home, standing on my kitchen shelf. It's the knowing that he would not be pouring some into a bowl everyday anymore that keeps me from buying it.

One of the foods Dovid liked was pancakes — not just eating them, but making them. When we lived in Israel, he made they from scratch and when we moved to America, he found a mix he liked. It became a kind of tradition in our household for him to make pancakes for us every Sunday morning. Even when he was sick and not interested in eating, he would try to keep up this tradition.

I had stopped making pancakes altogether. The memory of him working away in the kitchen was just too vivid and painful for me to deal with.

One day, on a shopping venture to the store, I found the pancake mix that he had liked so much on sale, and I decided to buy a box. The following Sunday morning I decided to surprise everyone with the pancakes for breakfast. I mixed the batter and started them sizzling on the griddle. I must have made almost a dozen when my oldest son Moshe came into the kitchen with a grin on his face.

He breathed in deeply and then said, "Mommy, it smells like Tatti in here."

I couldn't believe my ears because he was only four years old when his father passed away. "What did you say?" I asked.

Moshe repeated, "It smells like Tatti. Remember how he made pancakes for us every week?"

I told him that I did remember and as we began talking it came out that this was one of his only memories of his father — happily making and serving pancakes ("With tons of syrup!") every Sunday morning. My son and I decided to keep up this wonderful tradition. I wake him Sunday morning before the rest of the children and we make pancakes together. It brings back wonderful memories for the two of us.

*   *   *

It was nighttime and I was in my room listening to the quiet sounds of my four sleeping children. For some reason, I was feeling very calm. Something was different, but I couldn't quite place what it was. I tried reading, but I just couldn't concentrate. I went over all of the events of the day, but nothing seemed to have made a significant impact on me. It had been just a blessedly normal day.

Yet, I felt different somehow. And then, slowly, it dawned on me.

I had not cried today. I had not shed one single, solitary tear for twenty-four hours.

This may not sound like a big deal, but for me it was. I had been eight months pregnant with my fourth child when Dovid's illness was diagnosed. Then it was two and a half years of taking care of several small children and a sick husband, with many tears out of sheer exhaustion. In the last year of Dovid's life, I did not sleep through one night — out of fear and from his bouts of sickness at night — so I cried then, too. And after Dovid passed away, I missed him so very much that I could not stop my tears.

I wondered if I would ever get through a day again without crying. And now that day had come.

Yes, it had come, but it had also surprised me. I considered what this new development meant. It meant that I had reached a new level of acceptance of what had happened. I could actually smile again and feel happy with myself and the world.

I believe that tears are a wonderful thing — they express happiness and sadness and provide us with relief. But there comes a time when we have to stop and say, Enough.

It may seem like a small thing, but, believe me, to someone who has suffered a tragic loss, it is a giant step forward. And that was a step I was hoping to take — to move on with my life.

*   *   *

Every so often, out of the blue, I will have a strong reaction to something that stirs up memories of Dovid. I was helping out an hour a day with a friend who was critically ill, just holding her hand or rubbing her back and trying to get her to drink some liquids. A few days later I got one of the worst headaches that I ever had. Another time I saw a beautiful dance performed by a skater in tribute to her husband, who had passed away. It was so moving and powerful (especially the part where she spread out her hands toward the heavens, trying to reach him) that I literally could not shake the image from my mind for weeks. Once, a widowed friend happened to mention a song that made her think of her husband. When I finally heard that song, I could understand why she had that reaction. Now every time I hear that song, I automatically think of Dovid.

As the years continue to go by, I am amazed by how I can still have such strong reactions to things after spending so much time trying to build a heavy-duty retaining wall around my deepest feelings. But, somehow, something always triggers a reaction in my heart and the feelings that I have been suppressing erupt in full force.

I know that it is what I do with those feelings that really counts. So, I let them flow over me and realize that I have the right to feel sad sometimes. And then I make a conscious effort to put a smile on my face (even if I don't feel like it) and go out and face the world.

Chapter Two:

Do's and Don'ts for Hospital Visits, the Funeral, Shivah, and Thereafter

Whatever you volunteer to do for someone who is ill or for a family who has just lost a relative, you should do it just for the mitzvah. Do not expect any rewards for all of your efforts. Instead, thank Hashem every day that you are able to do a chesed, a kind act, and are not the one who needs the chesed done for him!

On the flip side of the coin, if there is someone ill in your family, remember to be appreciative of anyone who helps in any way. You should never feel hurt or insulted if someone does not pull his or her fair share of your load. After all, no one can know the full extent of another person's family, social, or work obligations. No one has the right to judge anyone else.

VISITING A SICK PERSON
IN THE HOSPITAL OR AT HOME

The Torah first teaches the importance of visiting the sick in *Parashas Vayeira*: "And the Lord appeared unto him" (*Bereishis* 15:1). Our Sages teach us that after Avraham Avinu's circumcision, he was weak and in a great deal of pain. Hashem did not send one of His ministering angels to visit Avraham, but rather, He went personally. From this we learn how important it is to visit a person who is ill.

When a person is hospitalized, he is there for one reason and one reason only — *he is sick.* (The exception to this, of course, is when a woman has just had a baby.) Chances are the person does not feel well and needs as much rest as possible to recuperate or just to preserve his strength.

For the family members, going back and forth to the hospital is unbelievably exhausting! And even if the person is at home, the parent or spouse must be on a twenty-four hour alert to make sure medicines are taken properly, no high temperatures develop, the patient eats and drinks properly to keep up his strength, etc. It is very taxing to keep up with either situation.

The following are ways in which you can help out a person in the hospital or at home at this critical time. These suggestions apply to relatives and close friends, as well as just acquaintances.

▶ Call first and ask if the patient would like to see visitors; and respect the answer you are given.

▶ When you go to visit someone in the hospital or at home, limit your visit to a few minutes. You can stay longer if the patient specifically asks you to spend more time with him, but even then, use your better judgment about when you should leave. When you visit, you do not want to tire the person out too much. Also, keep your phone conversations brief unless you feel certain that he really wants to have a longer conversation.

▶ If you find a "Do Not Disturb" sign on the patient's door, assume that it applies to you and simply leave a note to let the family know that you came by.

► Sometimes a spouse or a parent needs a break to go home and take care of things or, on the other hand, needs to stay in the hospital with the patient for longer than s/he anticipated. It is very hard to feel you have to be in two places at the same time. One thing you can do for that person is to let him know what hours you are available to stay with the patient at the hospital or to help take care of their family at home.

► Do not bring children along with you to visit. An exception to this rule is if you are visiting a parent or grandparent who specifically requests to see them. If the patient is too weak for children to visit, a nice gesture is to bring pictures of the family and, with the patient's and hospital's permission, put them on the walls near the bed, where they can easily be seen. Or, have the kids decorate colorful posters and hang them all over the room. They can also sing into a cassette recorder or just tell about their day, and this tape can then be enjoyed by the patient over and over again!

► How you speak to a person can either uplift or depress him. Do not talk "baby-talk" to an adult who is ill. Just because he is not well does not mean he is incapable of a normal conversation. He might not concentrate very well sometimes, but that can be just the effects of the medications he is taking. Or, his body may be fighting an illness, but his mind stays crystal clear. This holds true of many elderly patients.

► Do not speak to a family member in the room as though the patient isn't there. Don't speak about the patient in the third person ("How's he doing?"). Ask these things directly to the patient.

► The patient might look very different, especially if he has been undergoing medical treatments and you have not seen him for a few weeks. Because of how he is feeling and the different medications he is taking, his personality might be different too — i.e., he might not have such a long attention span, or he might be exceptionally quiet, or he might seem angry at what is happening to him.

Be prepared for all of these possibilities before you visit. If the person senses that you are uncomfortable around him, it will only depress him. Only go to visit if you think you'll be able to make good eye contact with the ill person, which is extremely important. What he needs the most is to be reassured that you will still treat him, talk to him, and look at him in the same way as before. Do not feel that you have to keep a conversation going with him or entertain him. Just go and listen to show your support.

▶ Someone who is hospitalized might really appreciate having her hand stroked or being given a gentle back massage. Because she is staying in the sterile, cold setting of a hospital room, giving her a light kiss or hug to greet her or when you say goodbye can really make her feel good.

However, it might be that her body aches because of the treatments she is receiving, and so she might be very sensitive to any form of physical contact. Even the smell of strong perfume or the sound of loud conversation might bother her. Wait for her to extend her hand to you first.

Even if there are no more chairs left in the room, do not sit on the patient's bed unless she specifically tells you to. Remember, you are there to make her feel more comfortable — not the other way around!

▶ If you are with a patient and someone comes in to perform a medical procedure or the doctor stops by, excuse yourself and leave the room. Doctors usually have time to see a patient only once during the day and there are many important issues that must be discussed then, i.e., how the patient is feeling, will she be needing any different medications, what the test results taken that day show, etc. Even if the technician or the doctor says that it is all right for you to stay in the room, your doing so will make the patient feel uncomfortable. Please give this person the privacy that he/she needs.

If you accidentally overhear some private issues being discussed about the patient, never, ever repeat what you heard to anyone. That information is highly personal and should not be shared with your spouse, your closest friend, the patient's relatives, or anyone else. Even if the patient has been given a "clean bill of health," what you overheard should still be kept to yourself.

▶ Do not discuss the patient's medical condition in his room when you think he is sleeping. He may just be resting, and your comments could really upset him. Also, do not underestimate what a young child can understand!

▶ Do not force a patient to speak to you about private or uncomfortable medical matters. If he wants to talk about anything and everything except why he is in the hospital, that is his prerogative.

▶ If the person is not allowed to eat certain foods, do not bring them along with you. And, of course, do not leave them in the hospital room, where the person will be tempted to eat them.

▶ On a Shabbos or a Festival, check ahead of time to see if the patient would like some company. Do not take a long walk to the hospital and expect to stay with the person until after Havdalah, at the conclusion of Shabbos or the Festival unless you have been specifically invited to stay that long. Otherwise it will be too much of a strain for him.

▶ If you know the person will only be hospitalized for one or two days, do not bring gifts to there, i.e., robes, pajamas, stuffed animals, etc. It will be a burden for the person to have to get these things home. Instead, send your gift or bring it to the person once she returns home. She will probably enjoy it much more once she is feeling better. Or just a card from you to let her know you are thinking of her is enough.

Flowers do add color and freshness to a room, but make it a small arrangement, i.e., one that fits inside a mug or a soup bowl. (One person told me that she had to make an extra trip back to the hospital just to bring home a large floral arrangement, because there was no room in the car with all her other things. She was afraid to leave it for the hospital staff because she knew that the people who sent it would be visiting her at home and they would be upset if they didn't see it there.)

If you nevertheless want to bring something with you to the hospital, then bring a particular book or magazine the person would like to read, or a special food that she is allowed to eat, or a particular tape she likes to listen to (if you know she has a cassette player in the hospital). Those things are very much appreciated.

Or, another novel idea is to bring something for the patient's nursing staff! More than anyone else, these dedicated professionals take care of your friend/relative and they truly deserve a little something extra. They enjoy getting home-made cookies, or donuts, or fruit baskets, or an assortment of bagels, and they have even been given pizzas! Put a note with it stating that you brought this gift because of the "good and special treatment" that they are giving your friend/relative. (Nurses also really appreciate having a note written about them and sent to the hospital administrator, reporting that they have done an exceptional job!)

▶ The above advice about not bringing gifts to the hospital certainly does not apply to a child/teenager who will be hospitalized for any length of time. That is something else entirely. If there is something you know the child/teenager would appreciate receiving, i.e., a certain item of clothing, or game, or book or crafts project, then it is appropriate to bring it to the hospital. (But do not bring anything that is too large or heavy.)

One mother of a sick child told me that a neighbor once brought him a "hospital gift box." Inside it were small toys, puzzles, coloring books, and games. The neighbor wrote a note saying that he should take out this box whenever his brothers and sisters came to visit him, so that they could play with these things together. The mother told me how much she appreciated this wonderful gift, because it made her son's hospital room less frightening to her other children. It became the "room where all the new toys are."

Also, most modern hospitals now have video players for the children to use. One young patient received an original video that his classmates had made especially for him. It was so funny that he played it over and over again!

▶ If you are bringing a present to a sick child at home, it is important to bring something small for the siblings too. It could be something to eat, like a dozen donuts or some ice cream bars or even a container filled with homemade cookies. The sick child's siblings should definitely not be forgotten!

▶ The best gift you can give someone who has a sick spouse or child is a card telling him/her that s/he is in your thoughts. I heard from many people how much comfort this gave them when they were going through a hard time. They read the supportive and caring words over and over again.

▶ When there is a sick child or adult in the family, the attention is usually focused on that person. The other children and healthy spouse often fall by the wayside. If you can think of a way to give them some Tender Loving Care as well, do it!

▶ The power of prayer should never, ever be overlooked. Make sure that a *Mi-Sheberach* prayer is said for the ill person in your synagogue. In the *Shemoneh Esrei* prayer, in the paragraph beginning with *Refa'enu*, there is a place where you can pray specifically for the person you know. Also, Psalms 20, 30, and parts of 119 should be said for the person. Other Psalms are recited according to the letters in the person's Hebrew name. If you are not familiar with how to do this, ask your Rabbi or someone who recites *Tehillim* on a regular basis to help you.

One woman told me that when her brother was in a serious car accident, all of the relatives gathered together in a corner of the waiting room and began saying *Tehillim*. She learned that another family was there for a similar situation, but they all sat around playing cards while waiting to hear how their relative was. The contrast made a big impression on her — how the other family dealt with the waiting by playing cards and how her family used the time as an opportunity to beseech Hashem with *Tehillim* to save her brother's life.

On a Personal Note: Once, when Dovid was in the hospital, the kids wanted me to constantly reassure them that their Tatti was being well taken care of. So, I told them to make a poster that said, "Take Care of this **Very Important Person!** He is our father." Then they glued photographs of themselves on it and decorated it. After I showed it to Dovid (who really got a kick out of it), we hung it on the door of his room. Everyone who saw it had a good laugh, and I can't help but think that the hospital staff took a little better care of Dovid because they saw those four adorable faces smiling at them!

Example: Miri* is a mother with a chronically ill child. She told me that when her child is hospitalized, she hardly

---

* All of the names mentioned from here on, except for my family members, are fictitious. The stories, of course, are all true.

ever leaves the hospital except to go home and shower once a day. Then she just flings some non-perishable food items into a bag and takes it to eat later. One time when her daughter was hospitalized, a friend of Miri's brought her a hot roast beef sandwich for lunch. Miri said that three years later she still can remember how good that sandwich smelled and tasted! She really appreciated getting something delicious to eat, instead of surviving on fruits, dry cereal, and granola bars! A hospitalized patient gets three meals a day, but the family members staying with him/her need nutritional food to eat, too.

THE FUNERAL AND SHIVAH

No matter how old we are, going to a funeral or paying a condolence visit is an unpleasant experience. It stirs up different emotions in each of us and many of us drag our feet as we go.

There is no correct way to react to the bad news, because it depends on the situation: Was it a casual acquaintance or a close relative? Was it an elderly person or a child? Was the person sick for many years or was it a sudden death, etc.? We all react differently depending on the person and the circumstances, but it is always hard in some way.

Yet, one thing was the same for everyone I spoke to: It was a tremendous comfort for them to see an outpouring of sympathy at the time of their great sorrow. Even if there are a lot of people at the funeral or making a *Shivah* call and the mourner is not able to acknowledge your presence at the time, still try to make every effort you can to go. It is appreciated more than words can say.

During the week of mourning, from the funeral until the end of *Shivah*, there are many things that people can do that will make this difficult time a bit easier for the mourners.

At the Funeral

▶ At the entrance of the funeral home, there is usually a book people sign that shows they were there. Please be sure to sign this book either before or after the *levayah*. There is so much going on at that time, and the mourners are so distraught that they, naturally, are not able to be sure of who attended. During *Shivah*, the mourners read this book and are comforted when they see all the people who made the effort to come to the *levayah* of their beloved family member.

▶ Make sure to turn off your cell phone. It can be very disturbing to hear that ringing noise while someone is giving a speech about the deceased.

▶ Regarding someone who has lost a spouse, be careful not to refer to him/her by his/her new marital status, i.e., "the widow/er." It can be horribly painful for the person to hear something like that — the equivalent of sticking a knife into the person's already aching heart. There is no reason to stop calling the remaining spouse by his/her name.

▶ When delivering a speech at the funeral, take into consideration the feelings of the immediate family. If you want to comfort the family members, remember that words are just as powerful and show just as much respect for the deceased when they are spoken in a calming voice. Very emotional, dramatic speeches only upset the family, especially grieving young children. Also, it is a very nice gesture for whoever is giving the *hesped* to say outright that he is addressing the children.

Of course, when a family member is giving a eulogy about a close relative (especially a child about a parent, or a parent about a child), it may be healthier to release these emotions than to bottle them up inside.

Note: When someone passes away, friends and relatives try as soon as possible to notify everyone they think might want to know about the funeral. Unfortunately, in order to pass the word around quickly, it has happened that poor judgment was used and a child or teenager answering the telephone was told to relay this bad news to their parents. What should have been done was to tell the child to have his/her parent call back right away in order to be told some "urgent" news. Or, tell them to not answer the next call and then leave a message on the parents' answering machine to call you back as soon as possible.

It Is Never Too Late to
Express Your Condolences

This point really must be stressed — there are no excuses for not contacting a person who has suffered a loss. He has no way of knowing that you are thinking about him if he doesn't hear from you. Once you make that *Shivah* call — either in person, by phone, or by sending a card — it alleviates any uncomfortable feeling either one of you might have when you see or speak to each other again.

Many people wait for the "right time" to contact a person who is going through hard times and often the "right time" never comes. Then it stretches on into weeks, months, and even years. This only makes for a very awkward situation when they finally do bump into each other. One person feels hurt and the other is consumed with guilt and remorse for not having been in contact sooner. As hard as it is, everyone should make a conscious effort to face an uncomfortable situation right away.

The whole possibility can be eliminated if you personally contact the person going through a crisis as soon as you hear about it. If you are not particularly close to this person, you do not have to show up on her doorstep one day to show your concern. Just call her on the phone and speak to her briefly. Or just send her a card to let her know that you are thinking of her. You can even buy a card with the message "Thinking of you" already printed inside and just sign your name. That's all there is to it! No extra words are necessary unless you particularly want to add a specific thought or message. That way, when you bump into this person someday (and you will!), you will not feel awkward at all.

The truth be told, there is really nothing you can say or write that will make mourners' emotional pain go away. But your demonstration of caring and concern can definitely help them get through this terrible time. Even if your phone call or card only makes them feel good for a few minutes — that is a few minutes less that they feel their overwhelming heartache. This applies whether you live down the block or thousands of miles away.

On a Personal Note: Many years ago I learned how important it was to make contact with a person going through a difficult situation. I had a friend who had been childless for many years. When she was finally blessed with children, I called to wish her a Mazal Tov.

"Where have you been all these years?" she asked.

Granted, we did not live in the same city, but I also didn't feel it was necessary to stay in touch with her. I answered her, "What do you mean, where was I? I was praying that you should be blessed with children all the time! I never forgot you!"

She answered me, "How was I supposed to know that? You never wrote or called once in all these years. I appreciate all of your prayers for me, but how was I supposed to know you didn't forget about me and my husband and our situation?"

That taught me a tremendous lesson. After I lost Dovid, when people came up to me and said that they were always thinking about me, I knew that it was true because I had done the same thing regarding this friend.

Now, whenever I hear of a critical situation involving someone I am not particularly close to, I try to either make a phone call or send a card or a meal, if needed. That way the person will definitely know that she is in my thoughts and prayers. Also, on my calendar I circle a day that is a month later to remind myself to give a quick follow-up phone call to see how she is doing.

The following expressions of condolence that I received still mean a great deal to me.

▶ On my bedroom dresser I keep a card that a very close friend sent me. The inscription on the card says: "Sometimes you must get tired of being both mom and dad...I think you're doing a wonderful job, though! You really are a terrific person, and I just know that everything is going to work out fine." When I received that card, it really brightened my day.

▶ About two years after Dovid passed away, I received a call from someone who had gone to yeshivah with him. The friend had just heard about Dovid, and he had immediately phoned me. We had a great conversation. He caught me up on the news about his wife and kids, and I told him how my children were doing. I didn't know this person very well, but I was touched that he had made the effort to call me.

▶ Right before the High Holidays (a year after Dovid had died), I answered the phone and heard this... "Becca, this is Naomi and I've wanted to call you all these months, but I just didn't know what to say and I said to myself that right before the Holidays I am going to call you and tell you how sorry I am about Dovid and I want to know if I can do anything for you — just name it!" All this was said in one breath followed by complete silence.

After a beat I said to her, "Do you feel better now?" She replied, "I feel great!" Then we had a good laugh and proceeded to talk for almost two hours.

▶ Dovid enjoyed cooking and baking whenever he had the chance. He always liked to try and improve on a recipe with a different spice or a new ingredient thrown in. Once when we were at someone's house for Shabbos, Dovid told another guest, Hadassah, about his fabulous mandelbroit cookies. Hadassah called me right after that Shabbos and asked for his recipe.

Almost a year after Dovid passed away, I got a phone call from Hadassah. She said she was hesitant to call, but she wanted me to know that she often made Dovid's mandelbroit cookies. I told her how much I appreciated her calling and how glad I was that his baking skills were still being enjoyed. Hadassah later surprised me by coming over with a plate of them, which my children and I really enjoyed!

Making a Shivah Call

As intensely emotional and hard as *Shivah* is, it is nevertheless a wonderful opportunity to relive the good memories that you have of the deceased person. I have walked into *Shivah* houses many times and have heard the sound of laughter instead of crying. The mourners were listening to a story about the deceased that they enjoyed hearing. It is not inappropriate when this happens. That is the whole purpose of *Shivah*: to talk about the deceased and to remember the good times with the sad.

It is much easier to fade into the background at a funeral than in a *Shivah* house. Yet, as uncomfortable as you may feel, it is important that you go even if it is just for a few minutes. Your expression of regret for the mourner's loss takes away a bit of his grief.

As a result of my conversation with many people who have sat *Shivah* for a relative, I have put together the following advice. For any halachic questions, contact your local Rabbi.

▶ Observe the mourner as you approach him and then you will know what you should do. Sometimes the mourner cannot bring himself to talk about his loss; sometimes the mourner talks nonstop. (Halachically, you should not speak to the mourner unless he speaks to you first.)

The purpose of *Shivah* is to set aside time for the mourner to grieve for his loss. Please let him do this. If the person is not in a talkative mood, let him sit quietly so that he can compose his feelings or thoughts. Do not think that you need to fill a void left by his silence. Endless chatter is certainly not appropriate. Don't try to distract the mourner with talk about other, mundane things. He can only concentrate fully on his loss at this time.

Follow the mourner's cue about whether you should talk or laugh or cry with him, or just be there to listen. The *Shivah* call is for the mourner's benefit, not yours.

▶ When a parent is sitting *Shivah*, invite the young children over to your house to play. Younger children are not comfortable when large groups of people they don't know come to their house. They find it frightening and disruptive. It helps if they can go to a friend's house (especially at *minyan* time, when the men gather together for daily prayer services).

▶ If you did not know the person who passed away very well, but you still want to pay a *Shivah* call, this is completely appropriate. You do not have to stay long, but when you arrive or when you leave, try to let the mourners know who you are, i.e., a friend of one of their children, a co-worker of the person who passed away, a member of the same synagogue, etc.

▶ It is inappropriate to bring babies to a *Shivah* house. It is very hard to talk about the deceased with everyone cooing over a newborn. If you can't get a babysitter, then make a short phone call or send a note instead.

▶ Usually, there is a sign posted on the front door of the *Shivah* house that says when *minyan* is and the time that the family will be eating breakfast, lunch, and supper. When it is time for prayers, the men are usually careful to arrive on time. The same consideration should apply to not disturbing the mourners during the mealtimes. *Shivah* is exhausting, and the mourners and their children need to have a peaceful meal in order to get through the next few hours.

I have heard of many cases where people just "dropped in for a minute" or refused to leave even when not-so-subtle hints were given that the family needed to eat. (One friend told me that it was two hours past the time the family was supposed to eat supper and no one was taking the hint to leave. She was feeling a little nauseous so she asked that her meal be given to her. As she started eating, one of the women seated there said to her, "Don't you feel a little funny eating in front of all of us?")

The person sitting *Shivah* should not be expected to play "the host" to everyone who comes to the house. People who come are there for a reason, not simply to visit. That is why it is important for there to be someone in charge at mealtime who will firmly but politely escort the mourners into the kitchen to eat, and stand watch at the door so that they won't be interrupted.

Women usually take turns performing this necessary task. They also supervise the quantity and types of food coming into the house and answer the phone.

If you are traveling from another city to pay a *Shivah* call, be sure to call ahead to find out when the family will be *davening* and eating. It is distressing to travel a long time, only to learn that the family's schedule conflicts with your own.

▶ When preparing a meal for a family sitting *Shivah*, simple food is the best. Remember, they have been sitting all day and have not been very active. Their bodies do not require heavy, rich foods.

Make it wholesome, nutritious, and delicious — just what they need. A friend told me that her husband was upset by the food sent for him during *Shivah* because it was as fancy as the food served at *Sheva Berachos* celebrations during the week following a wedding. His feeling was that he didn't usually eat that way and he felt uncomfortable eating such fancy meals while mourning the loss of his parent.

▶ Check with the person in charge of meals to find out exactly what the mourners need. Any food that goes into a *Shivah* house is not permitted to be brought back out again, so if there is no more room in the family's refrigerator or freezer for one more thing, bringing something without asking first presents a real problem.

Many times it is even more helpful to bring over a meal a week or two after *Shivah* is over. This is especially helpful to a widow or widower who is now living alone after the death of his/her spouse.

▶ Don't come too late at night. Even if you know the person sitting *Shivah* is a "night owl," he will be emotionally drained from the week and really in need of rest.

▶ If you come to a *Shivah* house and are told that the person you came to see is sleeping, do not insist that he be awakened. Just leave a note saying that you were there and express your condolences. Believe me, he will appreciate the note as much as the visit!

▶ If you wait until the last night to make a *Shivah* call, you will most likely find the mourners emotionally and physically drained. If this is the only day that you can see them, then by all means go. But, if at all possible, try to go as close to the fourth day of *Shivah* as possible. (Many people follow the custom of not paying a *Shivah* call until at least the fourth day, unless they are a relative or a very close friend.)

▶ If you live far away and cannot make a *Shivah* call in person, it is just as appropriate to make a short phone call. But when you call, know that the room might be filled with people and the mourner might not be able to talk. Just say the traditional formula for comforting mourners, "*HaMakom...*" and then tell the person that you will call him again in a few weeks. (A list of everyone who phones should be kept and written down for the mourners to see, since it might not be possible for them to speak to everyone who tries to reach them.)

Example: Marti sat *Shivah* for her father, who died at the age of ninety-two. It really bothered her that people kept saying to her, "At least he lived to a ripe old age." Marti said that those words did not comfort her.

"The message I felt people were giving me was that he was old and that it was time for him to go," Marti explained. "But I absolutely adored my father, and honestly, if he had lived for 120 years, it still would not have been enough for me. Losing a parent is losing a parent, no matter how old he is."

Example: Rita's teenage daughter passed away unexpectedly. One week she was an active high-school girl and the next week she became extremely ill and died within a few days. The *Shivah* house was full of people who were in shock, as were Rita and her husband.

Rita said that it was her daughter's friends who offered her the most solace. "For some reason, when a tragedy of this magnitude happens, adults search for something utterly profound to say, to make the mourner feel better. But the truth is that there is nothing anyone could possibly say that would alleviate my sorrow about losing my beloved daughter. Only my daughter's friends, in their innocence, were able to comfort me with their stories of things I wanted to remember and cherish about her. I was grateful that they did not look for things to say that would make 'the bad go away.'"

Note: Advice for children and teenagers making a *Shivah* call can be found in the chapter, "Children Have Very Different Needs and Require Different Treatment."

AFTER THE SHIVAH IS OVER

Death — funeral — *Shivah*. The stress and grief throughout it all can turn time into one big blur. For one week the family is coddled and looked after and then they are spit back into "real life," where the reality of their loss sinks in.

They are frightened and still grieving. They have hard adjustments to make and may look to you for some friendship and moral support for the next few months until they feel more stable.

People grieve in different ways. That is why it is preferable for you to wait until the other person brings up the subject of the departed first.

Some people may not want to talk about their loss for months. Others cannot speak about anything else. Be sensitive to their needs instead of forcing them to do or talk about something that you think is right for them.

They might need to constantly rehash the last few days their loved one was alive. A true friend during those hard months after *Shivah* is someone who doesn't mind hearing the same happy or sad stories over and over again. This is therapeutic for people who are grieving — to be able to express the tremendous sorrow they are experiencing and to relive the joyful times they spent together with their loved one.

Many people make a conscious effort to speak often about the person they lost so that he still can be a part of their lives. This may make others feel uncomfortable, but it is important — especially if children are involved. They need to know that dead doesn't mean forgotten. As time passes, it helps them to learn more about the parent or sibling they might have been too young to know well. In my house it was the most natural thing in the world for us to discuss what their Tatti's favorite cereal was, or what tapes he liked to listen to, or where he liked to study with his *chavrusa* (Torah study partner) at night, etc. I also asked guests ahead of time to try to mention a story about my husband in front of my children, if they had one.

The deceased's immediate family eventually learns how to cope and live with this tragic situation. But remember, just because a family is going on with their lives after a parent or a spouse or a child has died does not mean that they have forgotten the deceased person. They are just trying to return to some kind of normalcy as soon as they can manage it, which is, after all, the healthiest thing that they can do.

In general, it is very important to preserve memories of the deceased. When you phone to express your condolences, or send a sympathy card, or go over to visit, try to say what the person who died meant to you. Personal stories about the person are greatly appreciated.

I received letters from different friends and family members addressed to my children, telling them about their father. These letters are priceless. I make copies of them and give them to each of my children at the appropriate time.

Do not underestimate the value of letters or mementos to the person who has lost a loved one. One widow told me that a childhood friend of her husband's put together a small album of pictures that he had taken together with her husband throughout the years. She and her children had never seen many of the pictures in it before. Another widow told me that someone had sent her an old high-school yearbook that her husband was in, and she and her children really enjoyed looking at it. It is never too late to send these types of things to someone who has lost a child, a sibling, or even a best friend.

On a Personal Note: My children received a beautiful letter from one of Dovid's friends almost four years after Dovid passed away. The friend said that he had to wait until the pain he felt at losing Dovid subsided enough for him to be able to write down his memories.

Example: Ezra Garber lost his father when he was very young. At an engagement celebration for his older brother, a friend of the family took him and all of his siblings aside and said that he wanted them to know what a special man their father was. Then he proceeded to tell different stories about him, many that they had never heard before. This incident kindled Ezra's interest to learn more about his father, so he sent a letter to his father's family members and friends asking them for stories or pictures about him. He was so pleased when almost everyone responded to his letter!

In the first months following Shivah, let us...

▶ Cry!

▶ Reminisce constantly about the good times we had and our struggles together.

▶ Know for certain that you are sticking with us no matter how many times you hear our same stories!

▶ Know that you are thinking of our loved one too, and when it is appropriate, bring up his name in conversations.

▶ Express our emotions and do not try to stifle our anger, fear, worry, and sorrow.

▶ Decide who we want to be in close contact with.

▶ Know that we can call you anytime or, if it is a convenient time, drop in for a cup of coffee or a hug!

▶ Hear the toot of your horn as you take us a-w-a-y for a few hours to help us calm down and relax (in the country, a park, or a quiet restaurant).

▶ Show you our children's report cards or something we bought or something we made, since we have no other adult to share these things with now and it is important for us to continue sharing with someone.

We will eventually let go of your hand, but we will never, ever forget how you stood by our side when we needed you the most.

Good Things to Say

▶ "I was so sorry to hear about your loss."

▶ "If there is anything I can do, please don't hesitate to call, and I really mean that."

▶ "Even though I didn't know your husband/wife/child personally, I have heard such wonderful things about him from other people."

▶ "I hope it is of some comfort for you to know how highly regarded he was by all those who knew him."

▶ "You just lost your husband/wife and we just lost a close, dear friend. I know that the losses cannot be compared, but I want you to know that we miss him/her very much, too."

▶ "Don't think for a moment that anyone who will be at this (*bris*, Bar/Bas Mitzvah, wedding) has forgotten who won't be here with us. We want you to know that we will be thinking of him/her and missing him/her, too." (Said privately before the event.)

▶ "I can already see that your children are turning out to be wonderful like their father/mother was."

- ▶ "He will be greatly missed by all those who had the good fortune of knowing him."
- ▶ "Even though I just knew her for a little while, it was enough time for me to see what a nice person she was."
- ▶ "What I remember the most about him was his warm, friendly smile."
- ▶ "They say that time is the greatest healer. I want you to know that however long it takes, I am here for you."
- ▶ In a written note: "It was too hard for me to tell you what I really wanted to say, so that is why I'm sending you this card to express my feelings."

Chapter Three:

If You Don't Want to Cause More Pain, Be Careful of the Following

When a person is trying hard to keep her family together after a terrible loss, an unkind word or a show of disapproval concerning one of her decisions can undermine her and be devastating. Instead, give that person a smile and a hug, say an encouraging word, or tell her an uplifting story. That is a better way to help someone. It will send her on her way feeling good.

Read the stories in this chapter carefully and take them to heart.

What Not to Say

- "You look awful! Come on now, it's been a few months already! Go get some sleep!"
- "Don't worry so much. You'll get wrinkles!"
- "You were married for so many years! Stop looking so sad and be grateful for that."
- "Well, at least you won't have to spend all of your time now going to doctors' offices!"
- I know how difficult this must be for your children. We recently lost our *pet dog* and my kids took it very, very hard."

▶ "My husband travels out of town a lot and isn't always home to light the Chanukah menorah with our kids. What's the big deal about lighting the menorah alone?"

▶ "You think you have it bad! Why, ___ lost her husband when she was ___ years old and had ___ children. Did I ever tell you about the hard time she had?" (followed by all the details).

▶ "What's wrong with you? It's been a few years and you've already married off one child by yourself! Pull yourself together!"

On a Personal Note: During *Shivah*, one of Dovid's friends asked me, "Are you *sure* you got Dovid the best doctors?" I was, of course, shocked that someone could ask me such a question — especially during *Shivah*. Fortunately, I was able to look him straight in the eye and say, "The very best!" After being asked such a heartless question, I thought I would forever be prepared for any other insensitive question I might encounter. But a few years after Dovid's passing, I was taken aback by the question, "If you knew Dovid was going to die so young, would you still have married him?" I managed to get out a yes, but I was still completely dumbfounded that the person would ask something so ridiculous and personal.

BE CAREFUL ABOUT WHAT
YOU SAY TO CHILDLESS COUPLES

In the course of conducting interviews for this book, it was brought to my attention how often childless couples are besieged with prying questions and unwanted advice. If a Jewish couple is following an Orthodox lifestyle, then it can be assumed that they want to have children. Questions such as "*Nu*, so when are you going to start a family?" or "What's wrong?" are very personal and insensitive… and the answers are only the business of the couple's closest friends and family members.

If you are well-informed about a certain doctor or procedure that helped you or a friend/family member to conceive, you can approach the couple with the information that you want them to know, as long as it is done in a very considerate fashion. (Read "Supplying Useful Information" in the chapter entitled "Other Things That Are Important for You to Understand.") After that, let it go. It is up to the couple to decide what to do with your information. Maybe your information just isn't relevant to their situation, but they don't want to discuss the details of their situation with you. Do not call later and ask, "Did you go to the doctor I told you about? What did he say?"

DON'T SHUT US OUT OF YOUR LIFE

It is important for a person whose world is tumbling down around him as someone he loves enters the advanced stages of a disease, or dies, to know that the rest of the world isn't also filled with gloom and sorrow. Such a person actually thrives on being included in what is going on in other people's lives — where their days are more or less normal and hopefully devoid of major medical hardships.

In the darkest hours of my husband's medical crisis, how I welcomed the calls from family and friends who wanted to tell me about the little details in their lives or different things happening around town, such as a new store that was opening up soon, when an interesting *shiur* was being given, or what the next school fundraiser was going to be, etc. I especially loved it when a friend would call to tell me some good news in the community!

Because of the difficult situation I was going through, I knew that many times I was just too overwhelmed by my own troubles and fears to be there for anyone else. I am also sure that there were times when I monopolized the conversation, lamenting my unfortunate circumstances — especially when I was exhausted from attending to my husband's needs or overwhelmed by all that I had to take care of once *Shivah* was over. Yet, through it all I still very much cared about what was going on in my family's and friends' lives.

One lesson that we all eventually learn is that the "scale" upon which friendship is "weighed" cannot always be perfectly balanced. Sometimes it has to stay heavily tilted to one side for a while. During a crisis, our friends do most of the listening while we feel a strong need to unburden ourselves. What determines the strength of our friendships is how readily we change our roles to help each other as we go through both good times and bad.

After all, what is friendship all about except caring and sharing? Please continue the daily, weekly, or even monthly encounters that you always had with us. Let us know about what is happening in your life. It returns us to the outside world for a while and helps us remember what normal life is like.

Example: Chevie's daughter, Leah, lost a classmate in a tragic car accident. Chevie did not know what she should say to the girl's mother, Sara, and was tongue-tied when she made a *Shivah* call. She decided to send Sara a card expressing her condolences. When Chevie bumped into Sara in the grocery store a few weeks later, Sara told her how much she had appreciated the card.

Now, two years later, Leah became engaged and Chevie was making phone calls to invite people to the engagement celebration. Going over the list of whom to call, Chevie just could not bring herself to call and invite Sara, knowing that she would never have this happy occasion to share with her daughter. She felt that calling her would be like pouring salt on an open wound. After giving much thought to this dilemma, Chevie decided to write another note to Sara expressing how she felt and inviting her to the celebration.

On the day of the *vort*, Sara was one of the first people to arrive. She asked to speak to Chevie privately for a minute, so they went outside on the back porch. There, Sara told Chevie how much she had appreciated the note and the sentiment expressed in it. She said that although it was extremely hard for her and her husband to attend many of the celebrations involving her daughter's classmates, it still made them feel good to be invited because it showed that no one had forgotten about their daughter.

(Some parents who have lost a teenager or a young adult feel comforted when their friends make a concerted effort to keep in touch with them throughout the years. Other parents find it too painful to hear all about their child's friends, school activities, graduation rehearsals, future plans, etc. However, they do appreciate being invited to all of the family celebrations, even if they cannot bring themselves to attend.)

In an entirely different vein, the parents of a deceased married child usually want to keep up their ties with the remaining spouse and children. It is especially beneficial for the children. Later, should the widow/er decide s/he wants to remarry, it is important to discuss with one's future spouse one's intention to keep up this relationship. It is truly a blessing to find an individual who is understanding of this situation.

Unfortunately, there also have been heartbreaking cases where widows were completely shut out by their in-laws and their husband's family after he died. The family members hid behind the excuse of their loss being too hard on them emotionally. And so, they dealt with this loss by severely limiting their contact with the remaining spouse and children.

One of the widows whom this happened to and who was totally shocked by it said the following: "If my husband's family did not want to see me anymore, I could live with it; but it devastated my children. That was the hardest part of this to deal with — seeing my children in such emotional pain."

If you are considering estranging yourself from your grandchildren in such a family, please try to get some professional counseling. Such a drastic change is emotionally destructive to all the family members involved. Certainly it is hard to see the face of your grandchild who looks exactly like your deceased son, but it can also be an incredible comfort to see him living on in his child. At this time of sorrow, families should try to draw closer together instead of pulling apart.

BE CAREFUL WHICH STORIES YOU TELL

When we are living with a critically ill person and trapped in our own worst nightmare, do not add to our pain by telling us a story about how awful the disease really is. This is one of our main pet peeves. Why, when a person hears about our spouse being sick, does she feel compelled to tell us about a sister's husband's third cousin who had the same disease? Why must she then proceed to describe the suffering of that relative in vivid detail? This is horrible to listen to, especially when she gets to the ending!

Please think about the other person's feelings! Remember that useful information helps, but a graphic description of how the ill person will deteriorate over the years (as that relative did) is devastating for the listener. It is important that some standard of good judgment be observed here. And that applies to professionals such as therapists, social workers, doctors, and religious leaders, as well.

Sometimes a person will ask what can be expected as the disease progresses, but he may not be ready to hear everything in vivid detail. Such an answer, when he isn't fully prepared for it, can traumatize him. (A widow told me she suffered many sleepless nights after someone told her a particularly gruesome story about a side effect from one medication that, fortunately, her husband never even developed.)

Regarding the subject of inappropriate stories, there are some books that we who have lost a loved one avoid reading because their authors always include one story that centers around a family that is virtually destroyed by a member's illness. Also, we avoid certain speakers whose lectures invariably include at least one story about a "poor, unfortunate widow." One woman and her grown-up children refuse to go and hear an extremely popular storyteller who comes to her town every year. What offends them is that he always includes a story that depicts widows in an unfavorable way. We are offended by authors and speakers who include stories of this sort every single time. An uplifting story about how a family successfully used the different resources available to them in their time of need would be much better received and more helpful, too.

Example: Kayla's husband was diagnosed with a serious illness. At first, she told everyone and, as a result, was "treated" to countless stories about others who had the same illness or a form of it. After a while, Kayla learned to stop talking about it altogether.

Kayla's husband passed away a few years later without ever exhibiting any of the extreme symptoms people had told her about. She said that if she could turn the clock back, she never would have told so many people that her husband was sick, because the stories she heard frightened her terribly and made the whole situation much worse for her.

THINK BEFORE YOU SPEAK

When you are around a widow/er, you do not have to "walk on eggshells," but you should try and be careful of what you say. In this book, there are many cases of people opening their mouths only to insert their foot. At one time or another we all have probably done this unintentionally, but that still doesn't make it right.

There are many deeply painful things that can happen to a person in his lifetime, such as losing a spouse, child, young parent, or sibling; getting divorced; having a miscarriage (particularly upsetting for a childless couple); losing a child to crib death, etc. The list, unfortunately, is quite long. Don't ever say to such a person, "I know what you must be going through" if you have never been in their particular situation, because NO, NO, NO, you do NOT know what they are going through! Even a person who has experienced the same loss should be very careful about what she says.

Each individual has different thoughts, feelings, and ways that he deals with losing a loved one. Hashem created every one of us with our own unique emotional makeup, so it is just plain silly to group together all those people who have experienced the same sort of loss and expect all of them to have exactly the same thoughts and feelings about what happened.

Furthermore, do not think that you are helping anyone by making a statement like, "Why are you still so upset? I had a good friend who lost her husband, and right after the *Sheloshim* she picked herself up and got on with her life!" Please!

Everyone who has gone through a devastating loss has her own "personal time clock" for when she is once again able to deal with different issues and situations. Do not tell a person when she should stop grieving. You cannot expect one person to act the same as another. Certain people bounce back right away and then something comes up and they feel devastated once again. Others grieve for quite a while and then, suddenly, they pull out of it. You cannot tell a person how to feel. (Obviously, if the person becomes seriously depressed for an extended period of time, he may need professional counseling. But make sure the right family member or friend approaches him with this idea.)

We who have lost a loved one work hard to keep our feelings in check on a day-to-day basis. What we really need to hear the most is words of encouragement. We try not to dwell on the tactless things people say to us because we know that they were not said intentionally to hurt us. But it is exhausting to maintain a protective shield around our hearts all day long in order to avoid feeling hurt by someone's insensitive remark. We also cringe at being asked nosy questions about things that are personal.

Sensitivity is the operative word here. The old saying, "Sticks and stones can break my bones, but words can never hurt me" isn't true. Furthermore, sticks and stones can only hurt someone who's within throwing range, but hurtful words said to a person via the telephone can wound her even if she's thousands of miles away.

If you don't have something tactful to say, then don't say anything. Instead, when you see one of us, give us an encouraging smile, a thumbs-up sign, or a quick one-armed hug around our shoulders. Your good intentions definitely will be conveyed to us, even if you do not utter a word.

Example: One Purim, Debbi came to Shayna's house to bring her *shalach manos* (a festive Purim gift of food). When she saw Shayna, she said, "That's the new dress you were so excited about? I can't believe you bought it! It doesn't do a thing for you. Honestly, it doesn't look good on you at all." Needless to say, Shayna was so upset that she couldn't enjoy the rest of the holiday.

A few days later, after she had calmed down, Shayna told Debbi, "You know, if I had criticized something you were wearing, you would have gone straight to your husband and he would have made you feel better. Unfortunately, I lost my husband last year and can't go to him for comfort. So please be careful about what you say and when you say it. Purim is supposed to be a happy time."

Example: Sharon was hesitant to travel out of town with her children to attend a family wedding. She had recently lost her husband and this was the first celebration on his side of the family that she would be attending without him. Her children really wanted to see all their cousins, so she relented.

Her husband's family was extremely supportive of her and they gave her just the right amount of privacy and affection that she needed. The festive Shabbos before the wedding went well, and Sharon happily attended the wedding the next day, proud of how she was handling everything.

Before the ceremony began, an elderly woman came over to her and said in a loud, shrill voice, "You're Josh's widow, right? Aren't you his young widow?" Needless to say, Sharon was a bit stunned (and embarrassed), but she managed to nod her head in the affirmative.

The woman continued, "I thought you were the young widow. I just wanted to let you know that your husband was a very fine young man." The woman then gave Sharon a big smile and walked away. Needless to say, it took Sharon a while (in a room packed with people) to regain her composure.

(Sharon and I spoke about this at length and decided that age is no excuse for bad manners. The older woman could easily have asked a family member if she was Josh's widow and what her name was. Then her compliment would not have been tainted by the embarrassment she caused.)

Example: Evelyn and her husband were not able to have children of their own, so they adopted a brother and sister from a family that was unable to take care of them anymore. One day Evelyn was speaking with her childhood friend, Yehudis, and they jokingly tried to "one up" each other about who had suffered the most from ill-mannered comments about their lives — Evelyn concerning her infertility treatments or Yehudis about still looking for the "right one" even though she was in her mid-thirties.

After that conversation they decided to call each other whenever someone said something that really hurt them. Although their personal situations were vastly different, these two friends felt that they could really understand and be supportive of each other.

Example: Lisa had been a widow for two months when she met Rose at the grocery store. They knew each other because they belonged to the same synagogue. Rose was an older woman who had been widowed for many years.

Rose took Lisa aside and said to her, "I never got over losing my husband and neither will you!" Rose's comment absolutely floored Lisa.

"What kind of thing is that to say to a new, young widow?" Lisa lamented. "I heard her words and they seared my heart."

Example: Penina, a woman who was childless for many years and who adopted two children, told me the following: "The hardest thing for me was to meet a new person, because I knew that she would inevitably ask the question I dreaded answering, 'How many children do you have?' Unless a person offers you this information, this is one question you should never ask! You have no idea how painful it is to be asked and have to answer this question over and over again when you are childless. (I am sure that it is a hard question for couples who have lost a child, too.) It really makes attending celebrations and sitting at a table with people that you don't know, a very trying and uncomfortable experience. Believe it or not, there are a thousand other things that you can talk about except your children and your grandchildren. Everyone should try and make a conscious effort to be sensitive to our feelings. We would love to have children like everyone else. Don't make us feel worse."

On a Personal Note: The following story illustrates my "personal time clock" philosophy. I have a friend who tragically lost her husband a few years after I lost Dovid. A group of her friends were going to an annual convention that she and her husband usually attended, and I urged her to go. I thought that it would be great for her to be with all of her friends and "get away for a Shabbos." (Plus, in the back of my mind I was hoping that someone would offer her a *shidduch* [a prospective match].) She told me that she was just not up to it. I let the subject drop, but I was disappointed in her.

A few weeks later I attended a dinner in New York that was sponsored by my husband's yeshiva. I was really looking forward to going and seeing all of our old friends. They seated me at a table with the wives of Dovid's close friends, and they went out of their way to make me feel as comfortable as possible.

Nevertheless, about ten minutes into the meal I started feeling like I couldn't breathe. It felt like the room was swirling! I quickly excused myself and went out into a side hallway to try and catch my breath, but my heart continued pounding.

Just then, one of Dovid's former Rebbes, whom he had been extremely close to, approached me. (He might have seen me leaving the main room.) He said that even though everyone was enjoying himself at this dinner, I shouldn't think for one moment that anyone had forgotten who was not present this night. And then my tears began to fall. He stood with me for quite a while and gave me tremendous *chizuk* (encouragement) and, a little while later, I was able to happily rejoin my friends at our table.

As soon as I returned home, I went over to my friend's house and apologized profusely for trying to get her to go to a convention that she just wasn't ready for. I thought that, as a widow, I really knew what was best for my widowed friend. However, I had now learned first-hand a tremendous lesson about the importance of respecting an individual's decision regarding his own "personal time clock."

DON'T WORRY THAT YOUR WIDOWED FRIEND WILL BECOME COMPLETELY DEPENDENT ON YOU

Perhaps the hardest change in a person's life is being forced to go from being half of a couple and sharing a life with someone else, to becoming single again and having to do everything by oneself. When someone becomes a widow/er (especially when there are still children living at home), many adaptations have to be made in the way the household is run. It may seem at first that the widow/er is not capable of handling the change, but that is not the case at all. S/he is simply working out a new system of doing things that will keep all the family members feeling comfortable and cared for. Of course there will be much trial and error in the beginning, but eventually the kinks get worked out and everything calms down. People cannot be expected to readjust to such trauma in a day.

Anyone who has been widowed knows that the first few months go by in an incredible whirlwind. New things need to be taken care of while the family's routine needs to be maintained. Anything that family or friends can do to help during this transition period is usually appreciated. But, as close as you may be to the widow, do not try to force her to accept your help. If she refuses it, graciously accept her no as a no and try again some other time.

If you want to help someone in this situation, take the initiative and call first. Do not wait for the person to contact you because she will not want to inconvenience or bother you. She also will not want to feel greatly indebted to you. If you are diplomatic in your offer to help, it makes it so much easier for the person to accept. Do not ask, "Do you need anything at the store?" but instead say, "I'm on my way to the store. Can I get you anything while I'm there?" Or, instead of asking, "Would you like me to take Yona to the library?" say, "I'm taking my kids to the library this evening. Would Yona like to come along?" Saying things this way makes the person much more open to accepting your help because she doesn't feel that you are inconveniencing yourself for her.

The saying "Blood is thicker than water" is true for many. That is why some widow/ers opt to move back to where they have family. Family often translates into a reliable support system. Somehow it is easier to ask a relative for help than to ask a friend. But do not automatically assume that if the widow/er is living near family, they must be getting all the help and support they need. Check out the situation for yourself. (Also, you should not take for granted that a particular family's wealthy relatives are now supporting them. No one really knows another person's financial situation and the family might have incurred many extra expenses.)

Widows who are not living near any family might rely quite a bit on their friends during the first few months of their adjustment. As a result, their friends become their family. In many cases, widows are so thankful for all the kindnesses that these special people have shown them that they automatically include them in all of their family celebrations, both large and small.

People, in general, do not want to be takers. They would much rather be givers. However, after a person loses a loved one, the trauma is so great that s/he needs to take for a while before s/he can start to give back. If you feel that you might be able to assist a family during these first few extremely trying months, don't hesitate to do so. It is appreciated more than you know. (Refer to the "Helping Within Your Field of Expertise" section in the chapter "Things You Can Do to Help on a Regular Weekday.")

Example: Mrs. Charles was suddenly widowed in her mid-fifties. A few weeks after losing her husband, two of her friends called to say that they wanted to take her grocery shopping. She eagerly accepted their invitation, looking forward to enjoying their company during this little outing.

When they reached the grocery store, these friends parked and Mrs. Charles started to get out of the car. Noticing that they weren't moving, Mrs. Charles asked, "Aren't you two coming in to do some shopping?"

One of them replied, "No, we're going to wait for you here. You're alone now and you're just going to have to get used to doing things by yourself."

Mrs. Charles was so deeply hurt by this that she never got together with them again. (It should be noted here that neither of the women were widows. When Mrs. Charles told me this story, ten years after it happened, it was obvious that she was still upset by the incident.)

Example: Benzion noticed that his mother, Mirel, was particularly nice to a certain distant cousin of hers, Chaim. Whenever she saw him, she gave him a warm greeting and seemed to treat him with an unusual amount of respect. Knowing that this cousin and his family were not particularly close to her, one day Benzion decided to ask his mother about it. She replied, "Benzion, you were just a baby when your father died, so you don't remember much about those years. At the time, we were living a few blocks away from Chaim and his family. Until I remarried, every single morning for four years Chaim knocked on my door after shul to see how I was and to ask if we needed anything. *Chesed* (kindness) like that you never forget!"

BE CAREFUL ABOUT GIVING ADVICE TO SINGLE PARENTS

What particularly bothers newly single parents is how others automatically assume that because they are no longer married, this gives them the green light to go ahead and dispense advice about anything at any time. Nothing could be farther from the truth! Widows and widowers do not appreciate being told what they should or shouldn't do, the same as anyone else. We are shocked when acquaintances to whom we are not particularly close, insist on advising us about various things — particularly when it comes to raising our children! They seem to feel that since we no longer have a husband to discuss parenting issues with, they are helping us by becoming our "surrogate partner" in childrearing.

Of course, there ARE times when some good, solid advice concerning things that are outside of the parent's realm of expertise is definitely appreciated. If you are not close to the person you want to offer some information to, check with one of her better friends or a family member before calling her up. Let the third party decide whether your advice would be well-received. If you are given the "go ahead," then do not hesitate to call! Believe it or not, that's the way many close relationships are formed after the loss of a spouse.

Over the years, widows tend to form their own unofficial support group. They begin to phone each other regularly and are there for one another whenever they are needed. Yet even among themselves they are very careful about dispensing advice. Nobody appreciates having advice forced on them.

On a Personal Note: I was never part of any official widows support group per se, but I did grow closer to some women who were in a similar position — they had lost their husbands at a young age and had young children to raise. As we shared our joys and sorrows, we forged an unbelievably close bond, even though we acknowledged how sad it was that our friendships had developed because of our shared tragedies. As a result, we formed a "fictional Widows Club" which we joked was an exclusive private club, where we were not interested in gaining any new members.

Once I became a widow, I was asked from time to time to call women I didn't know whose husbands were ill or had recently passed away. I knew from experience that the wise thing to do was NOT to call them unless I was told that they absolutely wanted to hear from me. Otherwise I knew that they would consider it an intrusion on their privacy — which it is. I would only call if others assured me that the woman was extremely open to hearing from someone who had been in her situation before. And, even then, I would let her lead the conversation into the issues she specifically wanted to discuss. I remembered how several widows spoke to me after I lost my husband, and I used this as a guide in handling this difficult responsibility.

There is a fine line between making a useful suggestion and flat out telling someone what to do. If you decide to dispense advice, be very careful how you do it.

On a Personal Note: Bryna Cooper, a widow who lives in Baltimore, called me when she heard that Dovid was ill. I had never really spoken with her before, but I knew that she had lost her husband years ago and also had small children at that time.

The conversation was brief. She told me that if I ever needed to speak with her, she was there for me. I thanked her politely and hung up. I did not want to talk to her at that time, but I did appreciate the thoughtfulness of her phone call.

A few months later, in what were to be the last months of Dovid's life, I called her a few times to ask her advice on various issues concerning my husband and children. She never told me what to do. Instead, she told me how she handled similar situations that arose while she was tending to her sick husband and caring for her children at the same time. There were a lot of things that I could not bring myself to deal with ahead of time, but as each issue came up, she was there for me. Because she had "walked in my shoes" before me and lived through all the heartaches and pressure, and because she was considerate of how she spoke to me, I really listened when she answered my questions.

The morning Dovid passed away, Bryna was the only one I wanted to accompany me into the hospital's Intensive Care Unit because I knew I would not have to "put up a front" for her — she would completely understand what I was going through. To this day I treasure my friendship with her because she really listens to each of my concerns and does not dictate to me what I should do. She never makes me feel guilty about any decision that I have made, but instead, she encourages me to be my own person and to deal with my children in the way I feel is best for them.

DON'T PRESSURE A RECENT WIDOW/ER INTO MAKING RASH DECISIONS

When one spouse passes away, the surviving spouse should not be pressured into making any major life decisions. He does not have to move or switch jobs, put the children in another school, or start looking for another spouse etc. right away. He needs at least a year to restore his mental equilibrium.

Waiting to make an important decision does not mean that he is prolonging the period of mourning. On the contrary, it means that he wants to be calm and clear-headed before he makes a decision that will affect the family's well-being.

Surviving spouses may make some of the decisions listed above in less than a year. That is their prerogative. However, sometimes it may be apparent that they are making premature, impulsive decisions. If you see this and you are close to them, encourage them to talk their decisions through with someone they know and respect, who has only their family's interests at heart, such as a close friend, relative, Rabbi or Rebbetzin, or a grief counselor. Be sure you suggest this in a kind and gentle way. It is best done in person rather than over the phone so that they can see the real concern that you have for them. Try to visit them when their house is quiet, i.e., when their children are at school or in bed for the night.

On the other hand, a new widow/er may do certain things that seem impetuous, but really are not. He may have arrived at these decisions before the spouse passed away, or he may just be carrying out the wishes of his late wife. Perhaps the couple was dealing with the reality of the situation and planning ahead together for the family. This is definitely conceivable, especially if it was a good marriage.

Example: Gertie lost her husband very suddenly in a car accident. Her family began encouraging her to move back to her old hometown so that they could take of her and her children. Gertie was so overcome with grief and all of the seemingly insurmountable things that she now had to do alone, that she decided she would move closer to them.

One evening, a couple that she was very close to came over to see her. They spoke with Gertie for hours about not making any major decisions at this time. They told her that they and a group of her friends would give her all the support she needed so that she would not have to make any major changes in her life or the lives of her children right away. They wanted her to be able to make these kinds of decisions after things calmed down.

After that conversation, Gertie began to relax a little. She did not start asking her friends for more help than they were already giving her, but just knowing that they were there if she needed them was enough to relieve her of her feelings of being under enormous pressure.

After a year passed, Gertie decided not to move. She had gained new confidence in her ability to manage everything; and she also was able to think more clearly since her emotions were no longer in a turmoil. She decided that it would not be good for her children to have any more change in their lives at this point. Plus, she thought it was important for them to keep up the friendships they had forged with those who had been there for them during their year of mourning. She felt very grateful that her friends had encouraged her to take the time she needed to carefully think things over and to make the right decision for her family.

Example: After Laurie lost her husband, she went to visit relatives who lived a few hours away from her home. They lavished love upon her and her children and encouraged them to move closer. When it was time for Laurie to return home, it was very hard for her. She didn't know where it would be best for her and her children.

A few weeks after she returned home, Luba, who had been a young widow once but had since remarried, dropped by to see how she was doing. After Laurie told Luba about her dilemma — should she stay where her children had grown up or return to her hometown — Luba sat down with Laurie and asked her for a sheet of paper. She drew a line down the middle and labeled the two columns "Stay Here" and "Hometown." The two women thought of every conceivable advantage and disadvantage of each place and listed them carefully.

Once this was done, Laurie had a much clearer idea of what her decision should be. She decided to stay put for another two years until her youngest child graduated from high school. After that, she moved back home. Laurie said how much she appreciated Luba's sensible guidance at a time when she really would have preferred to "run home to Mommy."

Of course, there are strong, capable, and independent men and women who do decide that it would be best for them and their children to move closer to their parents right after they have suffered the loss of their spouse. This is a difficult and personal decision for anyone to make. Please give these people the time and the privacy to do so by themselves.

TELLING US ABOUT YOUR PAIN
DOESN'T ALLEVIATE OUR PAIN

Sometimes people think that if they tell us about their troubles or someone else's — i.e., marital problems, financial difficulties, trouble with teenage children, etc. — it will make us feel better about being widowed and somehow lighten our load.

Nothing could be farther from the truth! It pains us to hear that others are suffering. To learn that Mr. and Mrs. X are going through a rough time in their marriage does not make our single status any easier to bear.

If you have a valid reason for thinking that your very good, widowed friend can help you with a marital problem, then go to her for advice. (Make sure that you are not speaking *lashon ha-ra* — gossiping about or slandering another person — when you do this.) But do not purposely choose one of your widowed friends to talk to because you think your problems will make her feel fortunate that she does not have a husband anymore! (On several occasions women have actually come up to us [apparently thinking they would make us feel better] and said, "You are so lucky to be a widow!")

We really want our friendships to be a two-way street and to be able to share with others life's ups and downs. To offer an opinion or guidance on a particular matter or to just have someone with whom you can talk out a problem is what friendship is all about. Widows can and want to be included in that. But again, hearing about someone else's troubles in no way eases ours.

On a Personal Note: A few of the widows I interviewed told me that some of their married friends had let them know that their loss had actually helped to strengthen and improve their own marriages! In a most delicate and thoughtful way, these friends explained that after they saw how a particular widow was struggling to deal with everything on her own, they decided to stop nitpicking with their spouses on certain issues. Hearing this made the widows feel a bit better; they were happy to have contributed to someone else's domestic peace.

Chapter Four:

Other Things That Are Important for You to Understand

After consulting with a number of widows, I was able to put together the following discussion of important issues. Hopefully it will give you a better idea of how we are feeling at times, how to deal with us in certain situations, and what we do to keep ourselves in good shape mentally for our families. I would like to emphasize that not every widow thinks, feels, or behaves in the same way, so please do not assume that what is explained below holds true for each and every one of us. However, I still think that the information in this chapter will increase your awareness.

PRIVACY: RESPECTING AND PRESERVING IT

When it is discovered that a family member has a devastating illness, it is, without a doubt, a huge trauma for everyone involved. It takes a few weeks for the individuals to grasp what is happening, to know what to say to their children (young and adult alike), and to learn how to resume their day-to-day lives that are now overshadowed by the terrible news.

To complicate matters even further, they now have to deal with hospital stays and treatments, side effects to new medications or treatments, and medicines that must be taken according to a time schedule. Any one of these can be completely overwhelming.

This is why families need their privacy. They have to learn about the changes that they must make in their lives and determine what is the best course of action in dealing with all the issues that come up as a result of the illness.

One of the first things the family decides is whom to tell and whom not to tell. This select group of people will form the nucleus of the family's support system. Therefore, only very supportive people should be chosen — people who are truly concerned about the family's welfare.

The family may not want to let the rest of the world know about the diagnosis right away if the one who is fatally ill is expected to live for a few more years. On the other hand, if the prognosis is only for a few months, then the family might want to immediately inform everyone in order to rally *Tehillim* groups and to benefit from the prayers of others. Or, they still might want to preserve their privacy up until the end. This is a very personal and private decision.

There will always be those individuals who feel insulted that they were not informed about the illness early on. Their hurt feelings should not be taken into account. What is imperative is that the family, within the confines of taking care of an ill person, continues to try and have as normal and productive a life as possible. Their needs are of primary importance at this time.

The main guideline to follow in trying to help someone in this situation is to be supportive — not intrusive. I cannot stress the importance of this statement enough.

It is a wonderful when a person can make time for a friend or family member who is going through a personal crisis. A calm, supportive friend can quell the emotional or physical storm raging inside the distraught person. Yet, these people must keep in mind that even close friendships have their boundaries. Do not cross over the line of being a caring friend to being one who is a "tale-carrying" friend.

People will come to you when they need to talk things out if they feel you are trustworthy — i.e., they think that you would never repeat to others what they choose to confide to you. They will come to you if they think you will really listen to their fears and concerns — and also if they think you will never, ever try to pry more information out of them than they want to give.

"Being there" for a person does not mean that you need to know every detail about what is going on in the person's life. That is not true friendship. Sometimes things are just too painful to talk about. And if at one time or another your friend confides something really personal to you, do not automatically assume that she will want to discuss it even in the near future or ever again. Let her lead the conversation where she wants it to go. And needless to say, anything said in confidence should not be repeated to anyone else.

Also, if the family seems particularly hesitant about using a doctor that you suggest, don't press them for an explanation. They may not get along with that particular doctor, or they may have heard contrary information about him that they do not want to discuss with you. Their decision is a private one, but you can rest assured that they will go to the four corners of the earth to find the best place to treat the ill individual.

On a Personal Note: I got an urgent telephone call from a friend, Ruchama, who was very upset with her good friend Esty for seemingly shutting her and everyone else out of her life after her husband became ill with a serious, life-threatening illness. After all, Ruchama and her whole group of friends only wanted to help.

I explained that Esty and her husband were just trying to deal with their devastating news at this point; they had many important decisions to make and they still wanted to keep things quiet and stable for their children.

I explained to Ruchama that constantly calling or dropping over was only making things worse. Sending a card, a cake, a kugel, or flowers to say that they were thinking of Esty would be just fine, as long as they didn't expect to receive a reply.

Ruchama and her friends told me they were not happy with my suggestions and felt that they should do more. At this point I explained to them that they needed to redefine what "helping out" means. Friendship, I emphasized, means not making the other person have to deal with an onslaught of visitors and questions but, instead, being there for the person when and precisely in the way that s/he wants. Anything else is an invasion of privacy, no matter how well-meaning the person's intentions are.

After a few more phone calls, my message finally sunk in. The following week Ruchama dropped off a card and a cake at Esty's house. She was not asked to stay and she did not insist on coming in. Ruchama also started making short phone calls to Esty in the ensuing weeks just to ask if there was anything she needed at the grocery store, library, pharmacy, etc. She made it a point not to ask about Esty's husband's condition.

I told Ruchama that she did the noble thing, and some time later, when Esty needed to talk, I knew that she would feel comfortable in turning to her.

SUPPLYING USEFUL INFORMATION

It often happens that when word gets out about someone's illness, the family is deluged with advice from well-meaning family and friends. The suggestions and information that they have to offer can actually be useful in the following areas:

- ▶ Who are the top-rated doctors for that particular disease and where are they practicing?
- ▶ Which are the best local hospitals to go to for treatment?
- ▶ Exactly what does their insurance cover regarding treatments, hospital stays, and medicines?
- ▶ Where can they get financial help to cover their medical bills?
- ▶ Where can they find a competent therapist to help them or their children cope with this terrible crisis?

However, before conveying this information, it should be checked thoroughly for accuracy.

Such information can be obtained over the Internet, often by just typing the name of the disease into the search engine. It can take hours or even days to sort through all the information that turns up — and this is time that the family very well may not have. Assembling all this data and letting the family know what resources are available near them helps them tremendously.

But only do this research if you know for sure that the family would be receptive to it. In other words, you must be certain that they are not completely satisfied with how the family member's case is presently being handled. If they feel confident about the competency, medical skills, and course of treatment that their doctor is pursuing, there is no need to look further.

By no means should you undermine any of their decisions when they feel that the medical care they are getting is the best and right one for them. If you know of an excellent doctor in the field they need, or you've heard of a hospital where they are providing successful treatments, you can simply pass this information along to the family and let it go at that.

Keep in mind that you do not have to produce pages and pages of information in order to be helpful. You may have had a wonderful experience with a doctor or hospital and you want to pass that information along. Or, you may run across a short article that would be beneficial to them, such as state benefits they might be eligible to receive. That information is just as appreciated as doing hours of research on medical subjects.

The way you deliver this information is also important. Write or print it out for them instead of bombarding them with it when you happen to see them in the grocery store. They may not be able to concentrate on what you are saying at that moment.

If the information you want them to have is clearly typed or written in neat handwriting, they are much more likely to absorb the data when they look at it in the privacy of their own home. You can even write it down in a new notebook that has pockets on the sides for other information. Believe me, they will be very grateful to get it this way!

You can also send this information by e-mail or fax, but make sure the e-mail is sent to their private address and the fax has a cover sheet which lists them as the recipient. You can also send the information the old-fashioned way, by putting it in a manila envelope and delivering it to their door — whichever is most convenient for you. Do not forget to include your name, phone number, and address, so they will know where to reach you in case they want to get more information. If you are not close to a particular family, but have information that you feel is important for them to know, call a close family member of theirs and ask what is the best way for you to send the material you have to them.

Please keep in mind that the family may choose to handle their situation in a different way from what you have outlined in your research. There is no reason for you to get insulted if they decide not to take your recommendations. They will still be very appreciative of your good intentions and all the hard work you did in collecting and sending them information you thought was important for them to know.

Example: A couple took all of the information they gathered about their child's disease and put it on a computer diskette. Now, if they get a call from distraught parents who are facing the same medical situation, they just send them a copy of it or print out the information. Even though their child passed away, they update the information whenever possible as a way of helping others. It has become a family project in memory of their child.

On a Personal Note: I got a call from Sherry, who was upset that an acquaintance of hers, Rona, was seriously ill. Sherry was a practicing nurse who had worked in the hospital Rona was in, and she was well aware of how the doctors and nurses handled certain situations. It was her belief that Rona would not be getting the best care there, and Sherry did not know whether it was her place to say something.

I asked Sherry if she knew of a better hospital for Rona, and she did. She told me about one where the nurses and doctors were better educated about Rona's particular disease.

I advised Sherry to do the following: Put a brochure about the hospital and written information about the best doctor and nursing staff for Rona in a manila envelope and drop it by Rona's house. Also she should include a card saying that because of her nursing experience she felt it was important for this couple to have this information. And... take it no further. Rona's family would have to decide for themselves what options they wanted to pursue in her treatment.

Sherry was extremely receptive to what I had to say. I also told her it was a great kindness for her to do this for them — much better than going over to them empty-handed and telling them point-blank that the hospital they were using was not a good one for Rona.

ON LOSING A SPOUSE SUDDENLY OR AFTER A PROLONGED ILLNESS

While losing a spouse suddenly or after a prolonged illness are both very hard, there is a vast difference between them in terms of how prepared the remaining spouse is in handling the new circumstances.

After a Prolonged Illness

A woman who has lost her husband after taking care of him for years has slowly moved into the dominant role in their partnership. Over time she has assumed the majority of the household responsibilities, i.e., paying bills, maintaining the house and car, managing the children, etc. She has become extraordinarily adept at rearranging her schedule and that of her children at a moment's notice, since it was always possible that a medical crisis might arise. Once her husband dies, it is not as if she has been thrown into the wilderness without a map; she already knows how to manage things on her own.

But it should be understood that even though she has been the main caregiver in their family for the past few years and has shouldered all of the responsibilities, she still has to make a tremendous adjustment once she loses her husband. Although he could not offer much in the way of physical assistance, he still might have been offering suggestions regarding the children and finances, etc., and the wife still felt she was part of a couple — a team. Once her husband dies, she has to get used to being single in every respect.

One of the main problems this type of widow has to deal with once *Shivah* is over is pure exhaustion! Years of being her spouse's primary caregiver (and for some, also taking care of her children) finally take their toll. An emotional and physical fatigue can sweep over her so quickly and silently that she may not realize at first what has happened and why she is feeling so weary now that she actually has fewer responsibilities.

After a Sudden Death

When a woman suddenly loses her husband, adjusting to all the new demands that life makes on her while trying to deal with the shock of the death is completely overwhelming. After all, she had no warning and no opportunity to prepare herself.

One woman described her anguish over losing her husband in a fatal car accident with the following analogy: "It's like surfing on a tidal wave, trying to reach shore, but every time you get close to land another huge wave pushes you back again. And many times you feel that you have nothing to hang onto to keep you afloat."

A widow whose husband has died suddenly and unexpectedly loses her footing. It doesn't matter if her children are still living at home or have grown up and moved out of the house. She has to readjust the way she lives and thinks all at once and in every aspect. This is very difficult. After a few months, she usually is able to get her bearings again and settle into a schedule, but it takes time, a tremendous amount of effort, and unfailing support from family and friends.

Widowers

It goes without saying that a widower also has tremendous adjustments to make when he loses his wife, either after a prolonged illness or sudden death. If he has young children at home, he must arrange for childcare so that he can go to *minyan* and work, since in most families, usually it is the wife who manages the house and cares for the children so that the husband is free to go out and do these things.

Once the wife is gone, the world turns topsy-turvy for the husband and children. The husband may have to learn new skills such as food preparation, how to do the laundry and clean the house, and how to take care of his children's individual physical and emotional needs. He must make all of these adjustments while dealing with his own grief.

Whether husbands or wives have it worse is definitely not an issue here. Anyone who has lost a spouse under any circumstances suffers greatly. That is why people should please, please be extremely considerate when dealing with a widow/er who is emotionally and physically spent or in shock over the death of his/her spouse. Follow that person's lead as to what his/her immediate needs and wants are.

Note: Given that something could happen unexpectedly to either spouse, please read "Appendix Three: Expect the Best, but Prepare for the Worst," which discusses the importance of making a will, buying life insurance, and deciding who you would like to raise your children if, God forbid, something happens to both parents.

PEOPLE MAY EMERGE FROM SHIVAH CHANGED BY THEIR LOSS

When mourners step outside for the first time after *Shivah*, most of us notice that the world has stayed the same — after all, the sun has continued to rise in the east every morning and set in the west at night for those seven days — but we feel completely different. Our loss of a loved one has changed us.

As we reenter the "normal world" a bit unsteady, but determined, our friendships and priorities begin to shift. We draw closer to our counselors, seek guidance more often from our Rabbinic advisors, and consult with men and women who have been in our situation. We need them for their wisdom and experience; we have problems to solve and stories to share that only someone who has been in a similar situation can understand. As a result, this new circle of friends helps us gain trust in our judgment and confidence in our abilities. Our friendships of the past are not any less wanted or treasured, but now we need others who can help guide us into the future.

On a Personal Note: A few months after Dovid passed away, I received a call from Mrs. Ruthie Taub. Mrs. Taub had lost her husband a few years earlier. She was remarrying and moving to a different community and just wanted to say goodbye and wish me well.

Mrs. Taub's words of encouragement, advice on how to deal with people who did not really understand my situation, and on what my outlook on life should now be, made me feel so much better. She wasn't an old friend and she wasn't someone I would have come into contact with if I hadn't become a widow, but her display of friendship then meant a lot to me and was exactly what I needed.

"FIRST TIMES" AFTER SHIVAH ARE VERY HARD

It is really hard after *Shivah* to meet and greet people for the first time outside of the house. This applies to people who came during *Shivah* and more so to people who hadn't yet heard about what happened.

Many people who had suffered the loss of a close relative told me that for the first few months they would only go out in public if they had to, i.e., to run an essential errand, to go to work, or to buy food. They were worried about who they would see, the mutual embarrassment and the inevitable pain. One woman told me that she did not know what to say to parents who had recently lost their teenage son, so she ducked down a supermarket aisle and hid there until they left the store. Some people are able to make eye contact with those who have suffered a loss, but then they look embarrassed and very uncomfortable. They turn beet red and mutter something unintelligible and then quickly walk away. (Actually, people told me that they preferred that to being drawn into emotional scenes in public!)

While people who just lost someone they loved may be at a loss as to how to handle themselves in every social situation that might come up, those I spoke with all agreed that seeing someone completely avoid them often made them feel uneasy. And, believe it or not, many times they found themselves in situations where they had to make those awkward moments comfortable for the other person!

Perhaps this whole situation can be summarized by saying: You feel uneasy and they feel uneasy, but just a simple greeting and few kind words are all that are necessary when you meet anyone who has suffered a recent loss. Many times that is about all the person can handle. They don't like to be engaged in a long uncomfortable conversation about what happened — especially in public. (Refer to the "Good Things to Say" section at the end of the chapter "Do's and Don'ts for Hospital Visits, the Funeral, *Shivah* and Thereafter.")

Even the simplest routines are hard to return to after *Shivah,* such as attending the first *shiur,* the first *minyan* in shul, or the first P.T.A. meeting at a child's school, etc. Those who were mourning might prefer to sit in the back of the room for a while. Please understand that they need time to adjust to their reentry into even the most mundane of activities (even if it is something they've done hundreds of times and even if they were there just a week ago).

They may also need the emotional support of their family and friends to help get them through some family "firsts," i.e., holidays, birthdays, anniversaries, graduations, and other celebrations. Even though they are enveloped in the sadness that comes with not being able to share these occasions with the one they lost, they try to keep their spirits up for the sake of their children and the rest of the family and friends who, they know, are also suffering from their loss. Together, families should work to summon up the strength and fortitude to make these occasions happy times, as they ought to be.

After awhile, those who were mourning get their confidence back and comfortably face the world again. But, they appreciate it when family and friends let them do it according to their own "personal time clocks." (See the section called "Think Before You Speak" in the chapter, "If You Don't Want to Cause More Pain, Be Careful of the Following.")

On a Personal Note: I want to extend my heartfelt thanks to all of the wonderful, caring people who took my children to the pediatrician's office, did my grocery shopping, drove my car pools, or helped me with any of my other errands during my difficult first month after *Shivah*. Believe me, if someone could have gotten a haircut for me, I would have sent her!

My youngest child also helped me get through some tough situations, albeit unknowingly. I would carry on very animated conversations with him as I zoomed through the grocery store aisles (he was sitting in my shopping cart), especially if I thought anyone was considering approaching me. He acted as my shield, protecting me from something I wasn't yet ready for.

On Another Personal Note: After my husband passed away, I had to go to many agencies and such to switch our joint ownerships, policies, and accounts to my name alone. I always had to bring my husband's death certificate along and I hated doing this with a passion.

The first week I had to face this monumental task, my good friend Ashira Miller left her husband, children, and job for a week to stay with me. She accompanied me to as many agencies as we could cover in five days, and we really got things done. Whenever I was overcome with emotion, she told the person helping us, "Just ask me any questions you have! She'll sign whatever documents are necessary once we've finished." I am eternally grateful to Ashira for getting me through that first rough week!

On Still Another Personal Note: The first big milestone our family celebrated after Dovid's death was my daughter's Bas Mitzvah. Since she had been born in Israel, I wanted to make her celebration in our home with Israeli food and Israeli goody bags to give out, and I hired a teacher to teach the girls Israeli dancing. But for weeks ahead of time I just could not concentrate, because in the back of my mind I kept thinking about how Dovid would not be here with us.

I spent many hours talking on the phone with a friend, who was also a widow with a daughter having a Bas Mitzvah a few weeks before my daughter. Both of us were facing our first big family milestones without our husbands.

After my friend's daughter's Bas Mitzvah, she called to tell me how beautiful it was and how everything went so smoothly, without a single glitch. She was especially pleased that the speakers focused in on the occasion instead of making their speeches into eulogies for her husband. She had made it through her "first," and then she helped me make it through mine.

SINGLE PARENT FAMILIES: THE PHYSICAL, EMOTIONAL, AND LABELING ASPECTS

I like to use the analogy of the caterpillar and the butterfly when describing the process I went through from being part of a happily married couple to a single parent. A caterpillar suddenly wakes up one morning after living inside its nice, comfortable cocoon to discover that it has become a butterfly. The butterfly has just undergone a complete metamorphosis and, after I lost my husband, my whole life, too, underwent a major transformation. One treasured part of my life ended and I was left to meet the many challenges that now lay before me. Basically, I was the same person, but the change — with all of the new responsibilities it entailed — made me feel completely different.

The cocoon of marriage that I loved and cherished had been taken from me. Now I had to wrap myself in my new butterfly wings if I wanted to feel protected. They reminded me of the invisible helping hands of Hashem, always by my side.

I can also see this analogy holding true for someone who has lost a beloved parent, child, or best friend, or even for someone divorced who would have preferred to stay in the relationship and work things out. Suddenly she must face a life where the loved one is sorely missed and the pain of the loss is debilitating. But since becoming a single parent is the situation I am most knowledgeable about, that is what I will discuss here. However, I am sure that much of what I have to say here can be applied to other situations.

The Physical Aspect

Managing a household alone is difficult and exhausting — it's that plain and simple. The single parent must clean the house, do the laundry, pay the bills, maintain the car, fix the plumbing, take the kids to the doctor and dentist, make birthday parties, keep on top of each child's studies, get each child to school on time, help each one with school projects, buy them all shoes, clothing, and school books, take them for haircuts, etc., and still have a nutritious supper ready for them on time!

That is a huge task to accomplish for a full-time parent, but how does a working parent get everything done? As the saying goes, "When the going gets tough, the tough get going!" Single parents quickly learn the importance of prioritizing tasks, becoming very organized and efficient, and arranging for assistance when needed. Those who can afford it hire help. Those who can't, enlist their children, relatives, or neighbors when they need assistance. Often these people are more than happy to offer their services. Other times a trading or bartering of services can be worked out. All it takes is a bit of ingenuity and a positive attitude.

Most single parents try not to dwell on all of the work that single parenting entails. They feel very fortunate to have their children and pray every day for Hashem to give them the wisdom and strength to keep up with everyone's needs.

Example: Gitti, a single mother, had young children and a demanding part-time job. Fortunately, she also had a wonderful neighbor, Mrs. Mintz, whose children had already grown up and left home. A few days each month, Gitti would send her children down the block to the Mintz's house with a box of noodles and some vegetables. Mrs. Mintz then washed and cut up the vegetables and made the noodles for the children's supper while talking with them. She also put out board games for them to play. Gitti said that this gave her time to lie down for a while and regain her strength. It gave her the rest she so desperately needed before helping her children with their homework, giving them baths, and putting them to bed. She did not know what she would have done without Mrs. Mintz! To this day, Gitti and her children have a very close relationship with the Mintz family and they still joke about those boxes of noodles!

On a Personal Note: Lydia, a woman with three young children, told me how upset she was that her husband was going out of town for one Shabbos and she was going to be left alone with her kids. She was totally panicked and claimed that she didn't know how she was going to manage! Instead of showing my amusement, I gave her some concrete suggestions about how she and her children could enjoy their Shabbos alone together and she graciously thanked me. I cannot begin to describe the tremendous surge of confidence this gave me. After all, look who was helping whom!

On Another Personal Note: As my children grew older and joined more activities, I had to drive them to more places more often and I wasn't able to keep up with my friends as much as I wanted. One of my friends, Barbara, called me up after I hadn't returned her previous two phone calls and berated me. "Why don't you ever have the time to pick up the telephone and call me? I've called you a few times already! I'm not asking you to go out with me; I just want you to keep in touch. What are you so busy with?"

At the time, I was working extra hours before the Pesach crunch; I was preparing a *Sheva Berachos* celebration for one of my favorite helpers who was getting married; and I was driving my kids to birthday parties, Yiddle League, swimming lessons, Bas Mitzvah parties, etc. I did not tell her all of this, but I politely got off of the phone with her as quickly as I could.

A few days later, I saw my friend Shaindy — someone who was there for me throughout Dovid's illness. I could always count on her for anything. She had also left a few messages on my answering machine and I just did not have time to call her back. I felt so embarrassed because of what I had just gone through with Barbara that I didn't even want her to see me. But she did and she came right over to me and gave me a big hug! I told her that I had been so busy lately that I just hadn't found the time to return her phone calls.

"Don't worry about it, Becca, I understand," she graciously replied. "Everyone is so busy nowadays and you must be doubly busy being a single parent. I just wanted to let you know that I was thinking about you and missed seeing you!"

I walked away feeling so comforted.

The Emotional Aspect

Assuming full responsibility for a growing, active family puts a tremendous amount of strain on a widow/er. Those whom I interviewed told me that the most daunting part about becoming a single parent was learning how to cope with difficult situations and having to make critical decisions alone. It was frightening for them to realize that now there was no one else they could count on day or night beside themselves. Every single issue that came up, they had to face — alone.

Although it is a fact of life that pressing problems inevitably arise concerning the children, work, the car, money, etc. in everyone's family — and it can be overwhelming at times to deal with these along with all of the other daily responsibilities — the most emotionally difficult part of it is trying to decide alone how to handle everything correctly. It imposes a tremendous pressure on single parents. They feel that, with their children depending on them, they should do everything right every time.

Whenever they have to make a major decision, they often do the following:

- ▶ Consult an expert.
- ▶ Ask a close relative or friend for advice or just to listen to their concerns.
- ▶ Give the matter a lot of thought, knowing that — right or wrong — only they bear responsibility for the decision.

(When a couple decides together, at least they can share the blame!)

That is why it is so crucial for family and friends to express their support and even come out and say that they know these individuals are trying to do their best.

Single parents do not invite unsolicited advice, but if they do ask you for your opinion they are hoping that you will diplomatically steer them in the right direction, with only their family's best interests in mind. They are perfectly capable of making the decision on their own, but as it says in (*Mishlei* 1:5), "A wise man seeks counsel."

A married couple can bat around the pros and cons of an issue with each other. Someone who is single (whether widowed or divorced) does not have that option. When you are asked to express your opinion on a certain matter, try to appreciate that fact and take the person's feelings into consideration.

Feeling solely responsible for managing the household actually has ramifications in another area of our lives. If the garbage bag is still sitting by the door, or the bedroom is a mess, or we run out of milk, who is there to blame but ourselves? A tremendous lesson in marital harmony can be learned from this. How often do couples get upset with each other and squabble over these things? But when the option of blaming the other person isn't there, believe me, we all become much more tolerant and less judgmental of ourselves!

So whether single parents no longer have someone with whom to share the responsibilities or the decision-making — or even the blame — what it all boils down to is that they feel very alone and lonely. They might manage nicely one day and feel anxious and depressed the next. It takes a while for their emotions to stabilize.

It is also important to understand that even the full support of family and friends cannot alleviate the deep loneliness and the pain of loss. Someone can be busy from morning till night, but that "hole in his/her heart" still weighs heavily. It is tremendously hard to fill the void left by the death of a spouse if the marriage was good and the remaining spouse knows exactly what wonderful things s/he is missing out on as the days go by.

Sometimes fear and anxiety grip the individual late at night. A woman asks herself: Where will I get all the money I need? How can I be both a mother and a father to my children? Where should we live? What will happen to us? What will I do once my children leave home? Will I ever have a loving relationship with another man? Sometimes all these worries can make a person physically ill.

Yes, loneliness and anxiety can slash a zig-zag through single parents' hearts and their daily lives. Yet when they grow accustomed to and more secure with their new status — that was thrust upon them — they are able to slowly disentangle their emotions and learn for themselves the best ways to deal with the issues.

Note: In all of the many interviews done for this book, no widow or widower ever expressed any regret at letting that "one special person" into his/her life—even with all the pain and sorrow accompanying his/her untimely loss.

On a Personal Note: One night my young daughter came into my room and sat down on the end of my bed. She looked at the other, empty bed that was there and said to me, "Mommy, I feel so sorry for you. It must be lonely in here without Tatti."

I could not believe how, at her young age, she understood what I was feeling. I had always been very careful not to show any emotions like despair and anxiety that might frighten the children.

Then I realized that while on some level she was feeling bad for me, she was really expressing how much she missed seeing her father in his bed. I told her that, yes, it was lonely, but that I had beautiful memories and lovely pictures of her Tatti and her sister and brothers all around the bedroom to cheer me up.

That night she wanted me to read her an extra book before bedtime and hold her hand while she fell asleep. I was more than happy to comply. The human touch, even if only from the hand of a young child, really does take away much of the loneliness.

The Labeling Aspect

Sometimes people assume things about single-parent homes that simply are not true! They may think that our children must have behavioral problems, that our homes are filled with sadness, that our Shabbos and Yom Tov tables are depressing, and that we need advice on everything. Nothing could be farther from the truth! In most cases, it is just the opposite! Our children are normal and happy, our homes are cheerful, and we can handle our problems by ourselves.

I cannot count the number of times my children's teachers have told me, after praising their academic achievements or their behavior, "Mrs. Feldbaum, I just can't believe that your child comes from a single-parent home." This is of course intended as a compliment, but I am sensitive to underlying assumptions. Many of my single-parent friends have received similar "compliments."

Healthy single-parent homes provide a warm, loving, happy, safe, and supportive atmosphere where well-adjusted children thrive. Of course not every single-parent home is healthy, just like not every two-parent home is healthy, and not every two-parent home provides only wonderful things for their children.

To stereotype children from single-parent homes does them a tremendous disservice. It is even destructive. It undermines all the hard work these parents put into raising their children in a healthy fashion.

Example: A young, new widow learned this a few months after she lost her husband. She was waiting in the supermarket check-out line with her five-year-old daughter, when the little girl began to cry. "Poor thing!" this widow overheard. "Well, you know she comes from a single-parent home!" The woman was terribly upset by this comment, because her daughter's tired behavior had nothing to do with coming from a single-parent home and... all tired and impatient five-year-olds cry!

Of course, it is preferable to raise a family in a two-parent household! However, in studies conducted worldwide, statistics have shown that children who come from stable homes in which one parent has died have turned out to be very caring, exceptionally sensitive, and genuinely giving individuals. Because of the difficulties and adjustments the child had to go through when a parent died, s/he became more compassionate toward others and exhibited a greater appreciation of life than children who had not lost a parent.

The Jewish Observer devoted its entire Kislev 5760/November 1999 edition to the issue of, "Children on the Fringe... and Beyond." It examined the unfortunate crisis some families are experiencing with their children "dropping out" of yeshiva and rejecting their Orthodox lifestyle.

In "Report from Ground Zero," by Rabbi Yakov Horowitz, director of Agudath Israel's Project Y.E.S. (Youth Enrichment Services) program, he writes:

> For the record, I do not think that children from orphaned homes are included in the high-risk category. Aside from the pledge of the *Ribono Shel Olam* — the *Avi Hayesomim* [the Master of the

Universe — the Father of orphans] — to watch over His special children, anecdotal evidence would indicate that the overwhelming majority of *yesomim* (orphans) grow to become well-adjusted, very often outstanding young men and women. Fired in the crucible of the pain and loneliness of losing a parent, they often outgrow the inevitable "why me?" phase, mature earlier than their peers, are more sensitive human beings, and become exceptional spouses and parents, having learned at an early age to appreciate life to the fullest. And yes, they usually develop an incredibly close relationship with the surviving parent who raised and nurtured them under such difficult circumstances.

Just as an obviously handicapped individual strives relentlessly to be accepted for himself and not judged by his disability, we, too, as we maintain our single-parent families, strive to combat disparaging attitudes about ourselves and our children. In both cases the circumstances were decided by Hashem. We would like to cope with what He gave us without having our lives made more difficult by unfair assumptions.

On a Personal Note: I am grateful that my parents were never judgmental about these things. Had I been raised in such a prejudiced manner, I never would have married Dovid, whose parents were divorced. Then I would have missed out on sharing my life with this kind, thoughtful, generous, sweet, loving husband and father.

Example: This is an absolutely marvelous story I heard from an acquaintance! Raizy was blessed with a lot of children, and one of them (Rafael) has Down Syndrome. When a prospective match for Raizy's oldest daughter looked like it was getting serious, the young man's parents became very hesitant because of Rafael. Raizy told them the following: "What you see is what you get! We are proud of all of our children, including Rafael. What the outside world may perceive to be a blemish in our family, we, of course, perceive as just a child with special needs. Nothing is hidden in our family; our Rafael is out in the open for all to see! You can search and search until you think you've found the perfect blemish-free family, but let me save you a lot of time by telling you that no such thing exists."

MAKE A DATE TO SEE YOUR SINGLE FRIEND

When you know your single friend has a day of the week that is particularly difficult for him/her, or has a hard time being alone at night, or would love being included in your activities, your care and concern at such times can make all the difference. Some widow/ers find Sundays hard, when they must entertain their children alone all day long. Others don't like Mondays — the start of the school week or the work week. Some women can barely get through their Thursday preparations for Shabbos, while others are apprehensive of Fridays when they see their friends' husbands running errands or bringing flowers to their wives.

One widow described what Friday night is like for her:

> After I light the candles and Shabbos begins, my son goes off to shul holding the hand of my neighbor's husband. When he returns, I try to cheerfully say *Kiddush* and *HaMotzi*. We eat our meal alone on the winter nights when it is too cold to bundle up all the children in their coats and shlep them to someone else's house. Afterwards, I am hit by the intense quiet of those incredibly long nights once my children are in bed. No matter how hard I try not to, I always cry myself to sleep on Friday night!

Using a little ingenuity you can surely come up with ways to make their "dreaded day" a bit more bearable! Perhaps on Sundays you can invite them to your house to join you for a barbecue dinner, or even to a park where everyone can spend the afternoon riding on the bicycle trails or boating. To help with the Monday "blues," set a monthly date with your friend to go out to lunch or dinner. For the dreaded Thursday cooking and baking extravaganza, get together with her at her house and, over cups of coffee or cocoa, look over some recipe books for new, interesting recipes you think your families would enjoy. You can even bake together. On Friday, remember to call and wish the person a "good Shabbos." And on Friday nights, occasionally drop by for a visit. Those Friday night chats, without the kids or the phone interrupting, are the best. (Ask your friend if you can drop by anytime on Shabbos, or if she would prefer that you let her know ahead of time.)

Others told me that it was not the day of the week that mattered, but that they had a hard time with all of the evening hours. The blackness of night compared with the light of day can be depressing. The noise of the children eating dinner, doing their homework, taking their baths, and getting ready for bed fades into stark silence then. That is when the single parent is overcome by the knowledge that he/she has no partner to share the evening with, and those evenings seem to go on forever.

Some of these parents are too tired in the evening to think about their predicament, and they generally welcome the quiet. But there are other nights when these people would give anything for the sound of a friendly adult voice.

If you think this is true of your friend, make it a point to call her for a few minutes in the evening, just to check in. Hearing the sound of your voice will really make him/her feel better. And if she can manage to get out, suggest going shopping, eating out, or getting together with a few other friends, etc.

Also, do not forget to invite a widow/er whose children have already grown up and left home to go out with you

occasionally. S/he might still have a full- or part-time job during the week, or be busy with volunteer work in the community, but call and ask him/her to accompany you to a *shiur*,
or some other activity. It is so important not to forget about
this person. Also, be sure not to forget a widow/er who is
childless. You have no idea how much this courtesy means!

As infrequent as get-togethers may be — with everyone's
busy schedules and demands at home — the few times a
year that you are able to do to this means a lot. Also, do not
underestimate the importance of those brief phone calls.

On a Personal Note: One friend of mine, Perla Rabinowitz,
made a monthly date with me to come over while I did my
bills. That was something my husband had always taken
care of, and I found them hard to do alone. So, Perla would
chat with me for an hour or so while I organized the mail and
wrote out all the checks and — presto! — my bills got done.

Example: There was a *shiur* that Tova always enjoyed attending. However, after her husband passed away, Tova felt
awkward trying to arrange for a babysitter. She thought that
whichever girl she called would feel too uncomfortable to
refuse her, even if it was really not convenient for her to
come. She also felt that she might be putting the girls on the
spot: they might think they should be saying something to
her about her recent loss, etc. Tova felt so nervous about asking girls to babysit that she just stopped going to the *shiur*.

When one of Tova's friends found out about this, she
took it upon herself to find a sitter for her each week. Often
she asked her own older daughter to do this mitzvah. Tova
was very grateful to both of them, and she went back to attending the weekly *shiur* that she had really missed.

Example: A few months after her husband passed away,
Chaya's friend invited her to a concert where a popular Israeli singer would be performing. Chaya is a music teacher

and loves music. She wanted very badly to go to the concert, but she just couldn't bring herself to face people at such an enjoyable event. Her friend reminded her that she was no longer in *aveilus* (mourning), and that it would be very good for her to have an evening out. Chaya very hesitantly decided to go. Although it was very difficult for her to socialize before the performance began, the music really helped to boost her morale. She was very grateful to her friend for inviting her.

HOW TO KEEP A HAPPY OCCASION HAPPY

I had one stark realization after I lost Dovid: I will never feel completely happy at any family celebration ever again. That is a very bitter pill to swallow.

Once a family member dies, we are very aware of his/her absence at every happy event we attend. Friends and family rally around us so we won't feel so sad, but the aching in our hearts is a hard thing to ignore. The planning, the preparing, and finally, the day of the celebration all bring bittersweet pleasure.

People who have lost a beloved parent, spouse, child, or sibling say that it indeed casts a bit of a shadow over even the happiest of times. It is especially hard when everyone gathers together to snap some family pictures. Yet, the symbolism behind celebrating a *simchah* is that life goes on and happy milestones are reached along the way. Those who have suffered a loss still want to share the happy times together with the family and friends that they love, even though doing this is a bit difficult for them.

If you have a friend or family member who has suffered a loss and will be attending a happy event, you can:

▶ Call and ask if she needs anything for the occasion.

► Ask if you can perhaps lend her a fancy scarf, purse, or other article of clothing. Or else go out shopping with her. She might get a boost by the idea of wearing something new. Her whole attitude might even change about attending the event.

Example: Devorah had been a widow for a year and found attending family celebrations to be very difficult. Her grown children knew this and tried very hard to help her.

One day Devorah's oldest daughter, Batsheva, was in a shopping mall buying a pair of shoes for her son when she saw a dress in one of the store windows that she thought would be great for her mother. On impulse, she bought it and took it home. After packing the dress in a gift box and putting a colorful ribbon on top, she excitedly brought it over to her mother.

Needless to say, Devorah was very surprised to get this gift. She really liked it and when she tried it on, it only needed minor alterations. She wore it to the next family wedding and received so many compliments that her spirits began to lift and she felt less alone.

If a friend or family member has suffered a loss and is making a *simchah*, see if there is anything you can do to help with her preparations. Not only is this an emotionally hard time for her, but all of the preparations compound the amount of stress she is feeling.

You can help a close friend or family member who is going through this in the following ways:

► Send over a meal the week before the event.

► Invite the children over to your house sometime so the parent can run some last-minute errands.

► Invite the family over for a Shabbos meal a week or two before the event.

▶ If a wedding is being planned, offer to give one of the *Sheva Berachos* meals for the new bride and groom during the first week of their marriage.

▶ If the celebration is taking place at home, come early to help set up, or stay late to help clean up, or offer to help with some of the food preparation or serving.

▶ Come early to the house to help get the younger children ready.

▶ Offer to run errands.

▶ Offer to take the children to their haircut appointments.

▶ Try to be available the day of the event to pick up guests at the airport, or drive them to where they need to go, or take care of any last minute "emergencies."

Helping with any of the above suggestions will mean a great deal more to the person than even buying the most perfect gift for the occasion. After all, is there any more important gift you can give than being there for people when they need you the most?

Example: Bracha, a very organized and efficient person, was making a wedding for her daughter. For months she had been working with lists of what needed to be done and now the big day had finally arrived. Bracha's husband had passed away a year earlier, so now the responsibilities fell squarely on her shoulders.

In spite of all her planning, Bracha was terribly worried that she would not be able to get everything done in time. Suddenly the doorbell rang and there stood two of her good friends. As a surprise, they had cleared their schedules for the day and had come to her house to see what still needed doing for the wedding that evening. Normally not a very effusive person, Bracha threw her arms around both of them. Then, she put them to work!

The florist's car had broken down and she needed one of them to pick up the flower arrangements and deliver them to the synagogue. Her youngest daughter had somehow broken the heel of her shoe and needed to have it repaired. Plus, two of Bracha's cousins had decided at the last minute to come to the wedding; they needed to be picked up from the train station and they needed a place to stay for the night. Both of her friends were happy to help her out with these things.

Bracha said, "It didn't matter that I had a notebook to keep me organized. When the wedding day finally arrived, all kinds of unforeseen problems arose. I wasn't physically capable of handling everything. I don't know what I would have done without my friends!"

*   *   *

When you know that you and your friend will be going to the same *simchah*, be sure to call and ask if your friend wants to go with you. This gesture means so much. It is a tremendous relief for those who have gone or are going through a crisis to know that they do not have to drive to the *simchah* and enter the hall by themselves. They even find it awkward to leave alone. If you arrange to go with your friend, she will feel more comfortable and definitely have a better time.

Example: Varda planned to attend the Bar Mitzvah celebration of her close friend's son, which was being held at their house. She, a widow, arranged to give her children supper early and have them in pajamas before the babysitter came. All went well, and when the babysitter arrived, she quickly dressed and left. After pulling up near the house, Varda's heart started pounding. It suddenly dawned on her that all of her and her husband's friends would be there, and that this was the first time she would be going to such an event without him. She sat in her car and watched the couples she knew so well enter the house. She heard the music, the laughter, and the spontaneous singing coming from inside, and she just could not bring herself to open her car door and get out.

After sitting in her car for half an hour, she drove to a small shopping mall nearby and walked around before returning home. She resolved that the next time she was invited anywhere she would go with someone else.

*　　*　　*

It is not appropriate to discuss sensitive topics in the middle of a celebration. There is a time and a place for everything. People do not want to discuss their loss or be at the receiving end of pitying looks or words of condolence at what is supposed to be a happy occasion. Instead, make them feel good by complimenting them on how they look, or telling them the good things that are happening in your family, and be sure to ask how their families are. Help them along in their efforts to be and act happy. You don't need to hover around them. Just treat them normally and let them enjoy the *simchah*.

On a Personal Note: I was at Rina's daughter's wedding when Rina pulled me aside. She apologized and said that she did not want to ruin my good time but she needed to speak with me for a moment. Rina had lost her husband the year before, and she was trying valiantly to make all her family and guests feel comfortable and happy. However, instead of wishing her a Mazal Tov on the wedding, people were saying, "Oh, this affair must be so hard for you!"

"I know they're just trying to be kind," Rina said, "and I appreciate that, but oh, how I wish they'd just say how nice I look or that the food is tasty or that my grandchildren are cute! Tell me something to keep my spirits up!"

So I took her hand in mine and said, "Rina, you look so lovely! The smorgasbord is so delicious that I don't think I'll be able to eat the meal! And those adorable grandchildren of yours are really stealing the show!" She looked at me and we both burst out laughing! Then we went back to join everyone.

I knew that sitting down with her at that moment and lamenting the fact that we were husbandless would not do either of us any good. Nor did she need a lecture about how she should not take people's comments the wrong way. What she really needed was a light moment! And, I gave it to her. A good friend knows when to play it by ear.

Example: Bluma, a widow, was attending the second marriage of a close friend who had also lost her husband a few years earlier. They had been through a lot together and this was an emotional time for both of them. She was very happy for her friend and thrilled to be at her *simchah*.

Bluma said that during the whole evening, her friends were waiting on her hand and foot and repeatedly asking her if she was all right. She said that she was fine, but she was growing increasingly nervous because she felt like she was being examined under a microscope.

The final straw came when the bride appeared beside Bluma's table during the meal, poured some of the wine from the *kos shel berachah* into her cup and told her to pass it around the table so that everyone could drink from it. She started to do just that when someone called out, "No, Bluma should drink it all herself." She protested that it was for everyone, but to no avail.

So, feeling extremely embarrassed by now, Bluma recited the blessing over the wine and drank it while fourteen pairs of eyes watched her! (All of this went on in front of a woman who was childless at the time. She and the possibility that she might have wanted to drink from the *kos shel berachah* were entirely overlooked.)

*　　　*　　　*

At celebrations, the seating arrangements for older unmarrieds, widow/ers, and divorcees should be given careful consideration. It is preferable to seat them at the same table as their friends or relatives. If you are not sure who they would feel the most comfortable with, just call them and ask them.

It is never right to group older singles together at one table just because they don't have a spouse. This also applies whenever a husband or a wife cannot attend an affair and their spouse comes alone. These people want to sit where they will feel comfortable, the same as anyone else would. Keep in mind that people are individuals and not just their marital status!

Example: Judy was invited to a banquet that was being held to honor a good friend of hers. Having recently lost her husband, Judy was feeling very unsure about whether she should go, but a close friend of hers encouraged her to attend along with her and her husband.

When Judy and the Levines arrived at the banquet, they were surprised to find that the numbers on their seating cards were different. They had specifically written on their response cards that they wanted to sit together. They thought that they would be able to rectify the situation when they got into the dining room, but then they saw that the other seven couples at the Levines' table had all shown up.

Judy decided that she would sit wherever they had assigned her. She found her table and immediately noticed that everyone seated there was either widowed, divorced, or a single adult. She said to herself, "So this is where they're putting me now — not at my usual table with all of my friends, but at some table in the back of the room where only women without spouses sit!"

In fact, everyone at that table was uncomfortable because they really had nothing in common except their single status.

Judy felt upset and humiliated, and was so distraught that she couldn't eat a thing.

A Word to Men: At a *Kiddush* or at any large festive meal where *Kiddush* or *HaMotzi* needs to be recited, please offer to do so for a single woman or a family that doesn't have a male over the age of Bar Mitzvah. Women don't want to have to recite these blessings out loud and in public. If you see someone in this uncomfortable situation, please offer your services, even if you have already made or heard *Kiddush* yourself. And, at a large *seudah,* seat the woman or family where they will be automatically included when these blessings are recited by others at their table.

Note: As stated earlier, it is very hard to make a *simchah* after a close family member has died and will be sorely missed. That is why, whenever possible, others should make every effort to attend it.

When we hear that someone has died, we immediately rearrange our hectic schedule in order to attend the funeral. Or, if that is not possible, then we do whatever is necessary to be able to make a *Shivah* call. Yet, unfortunately, when it comes to celebrations, this is just not the case. People decide not to attend because the city where it is being held is "too cold" at that time of year or the kids will miss too much school, or it is too close to Pesach, or new clothes will have to be bought — excuses, excuses, excuses!

A friend of mine told me about her uncle who tries to attend all the family *simchah*s with his wife and children. She once asked him why he went out of his way to do this and he replied: "I don't want to be the relative that everyone just sees at funerals!"

Your presence at such a family's *simchah* is much appreciated. After all, life is too short...and who knows what tomorrow may bring!

THE IMPORTANCE OF THE
MENTAL HEALTH GETAWAY

The physical demands of raising young children or the emotional challenges of raising teenagers can become too much sometimes for a single parent. It is precisely then that these parents need to get away by themselves to recharge their mental batteries and regain their calm.

Many single parents take a vacation from their children at least once a year. Here are some examples of where they go: One travels across country every year to visit friends for a week, another attends out-of-town family celebrations alone a few times a year, and yet another, taking a very novel approach, sends all of her children to the Catskills to visit relatives for a week every summer while she stays home!

Single parents love their children and are "on call" for them all the time. It disturbs us when we hear someone say, "Oh, are you going out of town *again*?" Do not jump to conclusions about something you know nothing about. A sensible parent knows she must take care of herself so that she can take care of others. She will use her best judgment when deciding how long to be away, when is the best time to go, and which childcare arrangements will work.

All parents have to deal with their children's needs, wants, and issues on a daily basis. However, it is harder for a single parent because she must handle all these things alone; she no longer has a partner with whom to share the responsibilities. Short vacations definitely make a difference!

And remember, a happy parent is better equipped to raise happy children.

On a Personal Note: A few years after Dovid died, one of my closest friends, Tziporah Wachs, encouraged me to come and visit her and her family in Florida. They had extra airplane mileage points that had to be used up or lost, and Tziporah

wanted to use them on a ticket for me. After a lot of prod-
ding, I decided to go for a week. Inside I was very anxious —
was I wrong to leave the kids for so long? But I went and the
trip did wonders for me.

My children were waiting for me at the airport when I returned. When they first saw me, they appeared hesitant to
come up and greet me. I thought, "Oh, no, what have I done?
They must be really angry at me!" Then my oldest child came
over and said, "Mommy, is it really you? Why do you look
so dark?" They just didn't recognize me with my Florida tan!

Chapter Five

Things You Can Do to Help on a Regular Weekday

When we hear that a person in our community is ill, we automatically want to know what we can do to help him and his family — whether we know them well or not. Right from the beginning, however, we should honestly evaluate how much time we have to give so that we don't harm our own family. It is unlikely that we will be of help to anyone if we are frequently pulled in too many directions. Striking the perfect balance of how much to volunteer requires planning, like everything else in our lives.

SHOULD YOU BE HELPING OTHERS?

Ideally, helping others should be an integral part of each family's life. Whatever your children see you do will make a lasting impression on them. But, anything you choose to get involved in should be considered carefully.

Your family comes first and is your top priority! Whether you have babies or teenagers at home who need your attention, or a demanding job that is important to your family's financial security, or elderly parents who rely on you, they all take precedence over any outside commitments. What good is it to be busy with a synagogue or community project or helping out another family when your own family resents you because you're spending too much time away from them? Your *chesed* work needs to be planned around your family, your work responsibilities, and your physical capabilities — not vice versa.

So, always talk it over with your family before undertaking any community responsibilities. Becoming too involved in outside projects could be detrimental to what needs to be nurtured first — your marriage and your children. Remember, true *chesed* begins at home.

ASK BEFORE YOU HELP

The best way you can help anyone is to do what the person really needs— not what you think they need! This point cannot be emphasized enough. Many widows stressed this point to me over and over again — that although people had good intentions, they just were not being practical about the help they gave. For example, instead of automatically sending over a meal for the family, it might be better to ask if it would help more to take the children to your house for an hour so that the parent has some quiet time and can prepare food that the kids are familiar with.

Don't assume that you know what's best for a particular family, no matter how close a family member or a good friend you might be. They will be grateful that you were considerate enough to consult them first.

PROVIDING MEALS

So much revolves around food — Shabbos, all the Jewish holidays, and the celebration of special, happy occasions. Food also plays a role during sad times. For instance, the first

thing a mourner does after returning home from the ceme-
tery is to eat a hard-boiled egg. The roundness of the egg is
symbolic, reminding the mourner that life is like a circle, and
just as there are sad times there are also happy ones.

During the week of *Shivah,* meals are sent to the mourners'
house. In many communities, meals may even be sent to the
family for another week, month, or even months after, depending on their situation. Although meals can also be purchased from a kosher restaurant, the gesture of taking the
time to prepare home-cooked meals means much more to the
family receiving them.

For someone who has lost her husband, receiving supper
for a month after the funeral means one less thing the wife
has to worry about while settling her husband's affairs and
making other transitions. The nutritious food that is sent over
really helps keep up her strength. Often she is rushing around
so much trying to get everything in order, that she does not
take the time to sit down for breakfast or lunch. But many
widows told me that when the aroma of a hot, delicious meal
wafted through their front door at night, they sat down!

It is best if one person takes charge of organizing the
meals for a family who has someone ill at home or for the
week of *Shivah* or for a post-*Shivah* situation. That way the
following is supervised:

▶ The correct amount of food is sent over (it varies according to the number of family members and their ages)

▶ The family's standard of *kashrus* is observed

▶ The family's special needs are met (re: allergies, foods
they won't eat, etc.)

▶ The meals vary so the family doesn't eat the same
thing day after day

▶ The meals are delivered at the time that is best for the
family each day

It is also very helpful to send everything over in disposable pans. The less the family has to worry about, the better!

The following are a few "meal stories" that were told to me over the years. Hopefully they will start you thinking about the different ways you can help out a family when you send them a meal.

Example: After the *Shivah* for Naomi's mother was over, Lotty — her mother's best friend — came over and asked Naomi if she could see her mother's recipe book. Lotty then sat down with Naomi and asked which recipes there were the family's favorites. For months thereafter, this special woman sent over one supper a week using those recipes as her guide! Naomi said that she, her siblings, and her father really appreciated this thoughtful gesture.

Example: Karen happily recalled the time one of her neighbors, Beth, brought over hot dogs, french fries, and baked beans for her kids one evening. But for Karen, Beth brought a completely separate meal! "Beth gave me chicken, a baked potato, and a salad on a colorful plate with a matching napkin. She also provided a matching cup and my favorite Snapple drink to go with it!" Karen said. "It was so attractively arranged that I couldn't wait to sit down and eat it. And, believe me, I didn't mind missing out on the hot dogs in the least!"

Example: When it was Ronit's turn to prepare a meal for her friend Julie and her children, Ronit called Julie in the morning and told her to be ready at 5:00 P.M. because she was going to take them out to dinner. True to her word, Ronit came and picked them up in her car and brought them over to her house, where her husband made a delicious barbecue in their backyard. While the women shmoozed, the kids played ball or kept busy on the swing set. A great time was had by all!

"Not only did Ronit and her husband feed my family dinner that night," Julie explained, "but we all enjoyed their company as well! I knew that the kids were having fun, and I was finally able to relax and socialize for a few hours. And… no messy clean-up, either!"

Example: Zeeni is a very busy wife and mother, whose demanding career leaves her little time to spare. But on at least one Friday a month she brings Elana, whose husband tragically passed away, a scrumptious cake and delicious kugel. Elana told her not to bother, because she knows what a hectic life Zeeni leads. But Zeeni replied, "I feel bad that I don't have time to talk on the telephone and that I can't come over and help you out with anything. I want you to know, though, that when I bake for my family before Shabbos, I am always thinking of you. I really want to do something, and at least I can do this!"

Example: One day Aliza went to visit her widowed friend Shifra and handed her an envelope containing $100 worth of gift certificates from a pizza store! Shifra said that at the time she didn't realize how important those certificates were, but she soon found out.

"Some nights I was just too tired after working all day to make a nice supper, and I didn't have any money to spare to take the kids out to eat. So, I just pulled out my envelope of certificates and bought a pizza for the kids. We had cans of soda at home and I would pop some frozen french fries into the oven to go along with the pizza. Those certificates stretched for months. I don't know who appreciated them more — the kids or me!" (Note: This is a great idea for a family with children who are picky eaters.)

Example: A group of women wanted to help out their friend and neighbor, Tehilla, who had recently lost her husband. Although they could not commit themselves to making meals for her family during the week, since most of them had large families and hectic weekly schedules, they decided that they would prepare her Shabbos meals. Each week, two of them would divide up making her Friday night dinner and two others would prepare the Shabbos morning cholent and other dishes! One of them checked with Tehilla every Wednesday to find out if she was invited out for any of the Shabbos meals or if she would prefer to go to any of their houses for a meal instead.

Example: Fraidy and her husband Pinchas wanted to do something for Fraidy's close friend, Tamar, who was a widow left with two teenage girls and two teenage boys. Pinchas worked for a caterer, who was a very generous man, and he told him about Tamar and her family. Whenever there was extra food left over that Pinchas knew Tamar and her children would like, Pinchas' boss let him wrap it all up and take it all over to them. Tamar appreciated this so much, she said, because it never ceased to amaze her just how much hungry, growing teenagers could consume! It even happened, occasionally, that this boss would call Pinchas from an affair that he wasn't working at and tell him to come over and take the remaining food for Tamar's family!

Example: Another widow told me that a man who went to her synagogue and owned a chain of bagel stores would bring her fresh, hot bagels every few weeks. She and her kids really enjoyed making pizza bagels or putting tuna salad or lox and cream cheese on them.

HELP FROM TEENAGERS

Teenagers happen to be amazing! They are, without a doubt, an unbelievable source of "quality help." Being around their incredible energy and lively spirits is extremely infectious;

they offer single parents a breath of fresh air that we definitely need.

Whether part of an organized *chesed* project from school or just as one neighbor showing kindness to another, I didn't care how I got my helpers as long as they showed up! The teenagers who came to my home were a tremendous help and I greatly appreciated them.

The other widows I have spoken to all agreed: The teen volunteers lightened their workload, brought humor and laughter into their homes, and provided terrific examples to their children about what it means to be a *mensch*. They are a single parent's "ray of sunshine," especially during the evening hours!

Teenagers who want to help other families should:

▶ Be mature
▶ Be responsible
▶ Be careful to notify the parent as soon as possible if they will not be able to come over that week
▶ Have a cheery expression and manner no matter what situation they find, i.e., a messy kitchen and/or messy kids
▶ Be firm with the kids, making sure that the nighttime schedule runs as smoothly as possible.

A widow/er will need more help in the beginning, until things settle into a routine. Some of the widows I spoke to asked a teenager to come over for one hour every night to read to their children so that they could straighten up their kitchen and prepare lunches for the next day. Others preferred helpers to come over two nights a week for two hours at a time so that they could do the grocery shopping one night, and prepare for Shabbos the other. Knowing that they were going to have this free time during the week was a tremendous relief for them, especially when they needed to go out and take care of something. (By the way, the parent should also be considerate and tell the teenager not to come if any of the children have a contagious illness like a bad cold, flu, cough, etc.)

A teenager does not have to volunteer every week if her schedule is too hectic. Every other week or even once a month is just fine. But this volunteer work should be taken seriously since single parents really depend on it. Also, some teens do not feel comfortable going by themselves to a house where they do not know the family. It is perfectly acceptable to go together with a friend, as long as the job gets done and they do not spend the whole time socializing with each other. Even a brother/sister helper team is useful, but they should be careful not to engage in any sibling arguments in front of the kids. (After all, they are there to set a good example. They can save their squabbling for when they return home!)

Many teenage girls and boys came to help me and other widows I have known over the course of several years. They stopped coming only when they went to study in Israel, or left to attend a yeshiva, seminary, or university in another state, or married and moved out of town. Their dedication to the families they helped was way beyond the expectations of the widows involved. We all enjoyed watching them grow into outstanding young men and women. We encouraged our children — as they grew older — to keep up the friendships they had made with their teenage helpers, because we wanted them to always be close to these outstanding role models. They definitely enriched our children's lives.

Fortunately, we widows were able to return a favor or two to our teenage helpers. We gave them outstanding personal references whenever they applied for acceptance to a seminary or yeshiva; we helped them fill out application forms for the college programs they were interested in; and we also gave *shadchanim* (matchmakers) glowing reports about their character and sense of responsibility. (And, once they became engaged, we were the first in line to offer to make them *Sheva Berachos* celebrations!)

I don't think that these helpers fully understood the extent of the positive effect they had on our children and how much they helped me and my friends. Hopefully, now they and everyone else will know!

On a Personal Note: Just last night there was a knock on our front door. One of our all-time favorite helpers, Yocheved Gold, had dropped by to say hello. The kids were so excited to see her! The conversation, laughter, and comradeship between my children and her were beautiful to behold.

The following is a list of the ways that teenagers can help make a single parent's life much more relaxed during the evening hours. Please keep in mind that these suggestions also apply when there is someone ill at home.

$$* \qquad * \qquad *$$

Give the younger children their baths, especially during the summer months. After the hectic pace of a long summer day and the incredible amount of dirt and grime children manage to cover themselves with, once they are finally coerced into coming into the house, the parent is often too tired and busy to begin their baths! If a helper is willing to bathe the little ones, then the parent can lay out their pajamas and begin their bedtime routines. One mother told me that, to make sure that her children would cooperate when the helpers came, she saved certain bath toys for her children to use only then. It made bath time a special time for the kids, and the helpers really appreciated the kids' willingness.

$$* \qquad * \qquad *$$

Help the kids do their homework. Some teenagers specifically volunteer to do only this. This includes helping them with their school projects and taking them to the library if they need to research anything.

*   *   *

Play with the children in a manner that will distract them so that the parent can get some work done. If the kids are outside, the helper can play toss and catch or work in the garden with them. When the weather is not good, the helper can teach them board games. One woman told me how one of her helpers always brought along his "special" chess set so that he could teach the game to her kids, and she was delighted to see all of them turn into avid chess players. Another budding magician brought along his magic tricks and performed them once all her kids finished their homework. Still another helper taught the children how to weave potholders.

Example: A good snow meant big excitement at one mother's house. Her young boys would immediately call their helpers down the block and these teens would then come over and help her kids make the biggest snowman on the block or the longest ice fort. And, while working on those, they would also graciously shovel a path from her front door to the sidewalk and clear off her car. (But the teenagers made the boys promise not to call them too early if school was canceled for the day!)

*   *   *

Help with the housework. Some volunteers prefer to do this and not to interact with the children at all. They may be much more comfortable folding laundry, washing the supper dishes, straightening up, etc. This is just fine, since many parents prefer to watch their own children and leave the housework to someone else. (Parents, please note: If a helper offers to do household chores, ask what s/he prefers to do. Don't use helpers as a housecleaning service or, believe me, that will be the last time you ever see them!)

Example: One woman told me about the time she had an important meeting to attend and she had to leave her helper with a messy house. She apologized profusely and instructed her to just get her kids to bed and to please ignore how the house looked; she would straighten it up once she got home. Well, when she came back, she was startled to see the condition her house was in. It was completely cleaned up! (She felt like stepping outside to check that she was at the right address!) This helper had realized that the mother, a recent widow, could use some extra help this time. So she had asked her best friend to come over and they took turns watching the children and straightening up the house. This mother said their generosity lifted her spirits for the entire week.

Example: Laura, a mother with an ill child, could not praise her helpers enough. "I really felt that the teenagers who came over to help us brought light and happiness along with them. Whenever they came into my home, they automatically assessed the situation and just knew what to do, like give the kids baths, or put a load of laundry into the washing machine, or even hold my sick child in their arms and softly rock and sing to him when he wasn't feeling well. Many times, after a difficult week, they were the ones who kept me grounded."

Example: One teenager had a very hectic school and work schedule, but she also wanted to help a certain family on her block. And so on Thursday nights, when she went food shopping for her mother, she began to take along a different child each week from that family. The mother really appreciated this: it was a treat for the child and it also helped her since there was always some grocery item she had forgotten to buy.

*   *   *

Help on Shabbos if that's better for you. Some volunteers come after candle lighting on Friday evenings to read to the children or to take them out for a walk. Others prefer to take the children to their Bnos or Pirchei groups and then watch them afterwards so that their parent can get some well-deserved rest!

Example: Bayla had been a helper at the Goldman family's house for many years. When it became impossible for her to come during the evenings anymore, she came to them every Friday afternoon to blow-dry and style the girls' hair! Bayla had done this for so many years when they were little, and she still enjoyed doing it now that they were teenagers! The girls really looked forward to seeing her and enjoyed their fancy hairstyles in honor of Shabbos.

On a Personal Note: In my opinion, the happiest children come from homes where they see acts of *chesed* being performed for others. It has an everlasting effect on them. Also, when children realize they have the ability to cheer up another human being, it builds their sense of self-worth. I know families who encourage their children to play with children who are handicapped or to do homework with kids who have lost a parent or to take a child with a sick sibling to a ballgame. The possibilities are endless.

However, this only works if the parents understand that their child's schoolwork and extracurricular activities come first. That way the child will not feel any pressure when he volunteers, because he already will have taken care of his personal business. He should be taught that only after he sees to his own responsibilities can he be a good role model and a help to someone else.

Also, parents should never volunteer their children to help someone without asking them first. *Chesed* should be something they look forward to doing — not a drudgery.

*   *   *

Much heartfelt thanks and gratitude is due to those wonderful parents who encourage their sons and daughters to help others. These special young men and women will become caring and giving adults, who in turn will be a source of great pride to their parents and their communities.

On a Personal Note: An acquaintance of mine, Robin, heard that my husband was very ill. She called me and offered to send her teenage daughters over to help out on Thursday nights. I was hesitant to accept and Robin sensed my discomfort. I told Robin that some days it was not so pleasant around my home with a nurse or doctor coming, or the rooms messy, or the atmosphere tense.

I will never forget the following words Robin said to me: "I want my daughters to grow up knowing that life is not just fun and games. They'll have to learn about the real world sooner or later, and I would rather it be sooner than later!"

I told Robin how much I really could use the extra pairs of hands, but I only wanted her daughters to come over on the condition that she carefully explain the situation to them and let them decide on their own. Robin promised me she would.

Well, as the saying goes, the apple doesn't fall far from the tree! Robin's daughters gladly came over to help on Thursday nights and it was a wonderful relief for me.

My husband made it a point to thank these girls whenever they came and my kids really looked forward to seeing them too. (These girls continued to help out until they graduated from high school, and to this day, they still keep in contact with my children.)

This is what we should all strive for: to raise sensitive individuals who respond when another is in need. And just think what wonderful husbands and wives these helpers will turn out to be!

On Another Personal Note: In the chapter "Things You Can Do to Help on the Sabbath and the Festivals," I mention that when my children came down with the chicken pox a few weeks after my husband passed away, some people brought presents over for them. One of them was Nechama Solomon. I hardly knew her, but our daughters were acquaintances in school and camp. We hit it off and, being the terrific cook that she is, she brought over some soup or a kugel or a cake from time to time.

As it turned out, her grandfather, Eliezer Rubin, had given my grandmother — who was raising five children alone at the time — all the emotional and (at times) the financial support she needed for many years. I had grown up hearing my mother say that she did not know how her mother would have gotten through the tough times without him.

Upon learning of this connection, Nechama and I formed a special bond and have become close friends. It convinced me that the practice of *chesed* is passed down from generation to generation in some families.

BIKKUR CHOLIM

If you want to help people deal with a medical crisis in their family, but you don't know who could use you or exactly how to assist, you can always volunteer at your local Bikkur Cholim organization. These have been founded in many Jewish communities around the world. They serve as a clearinghouse of information: Who needs help? What help do they need? Where else can these people go for other kinds of help they might need? They also coordinate volunteers' services so that these families' needs are met.

Family members can begin to feel like their whole lives are revolving around the illness that has invaded their home and they become isolated from those family and friends whose lives are continuing along just as they used to. The daily stress of tending to a sick person and making crucial decisions can overwhelm them. Things around the house begin to fall by the wayside, and the children might start feeling neglected. Meanwhile, the adults are struggling with the medical bills, the hourly needs of the sick person, job obligations, and maintaining some sort of order at home. A Bikkur Cholim organization can reach out and help them with just these responsibilities.

In smaller Jewish communities, many Bikkur Cholims are run by the Sisterhood or the Men's Club of a synagogue. In larger Jewish communities, the Bikkur Cholims may have separate branches because, unfortunately, the needs of the community are so vast. One branch might take care of the needs of hospitalized patients, another the needs of the ill who are at home and their families, while another might help with their financial situation, etc.

In some cities, all of the Bikkur Cholim volunteers who visit hospital patients or help out their families are required to attend a fixed number of lectures given by an experienced psychologist and a grief therapist. These professionals teach the volunteers the "do's and don'ts" of dealing with an ill person and his family.

Many of these organizations assign a volunteer to each family to ascertain what they need on a weekly or monthly basis. Each family's needs have to be individually evaluated because every family is different (i.e., there may be young children to take care of, the infirm person might be living alone, there may not be other family members in the city, etc.)

Of course, the family's boundaries need to be respected. Help is always appreciated, but too much is an invasion. No one wants to be considered a pathetic case. The recipients have to have the final say in what is going on in their own homes. They should feel that the Bikkur Cholim is an extended part of their family, not an organization that is meddlesome and annoying.

Volunteers must be scrupulous not to tell others whom they are helping or any confidential medical information they might be privy to. What makes these organizations so successful is their high standard of professionalism. People feel that they can trust everyone affiliated with Bikkur Cholim to treat them in a respectful manner and to hold anything private about them in the strictest of confidence.

When you call a Bikkur Cholim organization to volunteer some of your time, ask exactly what services they provide for your community. That way, you can choose which activities you would like to join and see what fits into your schedule the best. If you think you would feel awkward going into someone's house to help out or visiting someone you don't know in the hospital, there are many other things you can do, such as helping to prepare meals, or making telephone calls, or putting together Shabbos packages, etc. (See the list below.)

The good thing about volunteering for such an organization is that there are a myriad of things that are needed; you can always find an outlet for your special abilities that will do some good. Also, by being involved in Bikkur Cholim activities, you will show your children what the word *chesed* really means.

Example: Fern lost her husband after an illness that lasted many, many years. She had a part-time job and teenagers at home who needed her time and attention, but she nevertheless made it a point to devote a few hours a week to her local Bikkur Cholim. Someone once asked her how she was able to go back to the hospital and visit patients when she had already spent so many years there.

She replied, "The Bikkur Cholim in my community was there for me all those years when my husband was ill, and they were unbelievably supportive. Yes, it definitely is hard at times for me to walk those hospital corridors. But I know how important it is to see the friendly face of someone who isn't wearing a white uniform or a stethoscope. So, when people ask me how I can do it, I like to reply, 'How can I not?'"

Ways That Bikkur Cholim Helps

If you need to go to a medical center for treatment that is located in another city, call ahead to the Bikkur Cholim there. In many cities that have a major medical center and a large Jewish population, special services are provided for patients and their families coming in from another state or country.

Listed below are some ways in which Bikkur Cholim organizations assist people:

▶ **Transportation.** This includes driving patients and their family to and from doctors' offices, bringing them meals, picking up prescriptions for them, chauffeuring family members to their activities, delivering Shabbos flowers or packages to them, driving a car pool for them.

▶ **Meals.** Many women find this an easy way to help out, since they simply double whatever they are cooking for their own families. One Bikkur Cholim organization I am familiar with lends freezers to families and fills them with two weeks' worth of cooked, labeled meals. That way, the food is already in the house, available to meet the family's needs. (Read the "Providing Meals" section in this chapter.)

Some patients are on a restricted diet and may have special food needs, such as: no milk products, no gluten, macrobiotic cooking, vegetarian meals, no sugar, no salt, no food coloring, etc. People who are used to cooking in compliance with these food restrictions can help out by making extra meals for the Bikkur Cholim. The food they prepare will taste much better than that prepared by others, because they already have experience substituting permissible ingredients to enhance its flavor.

▶ **Home Visits.** An elderly person who is ill and housebound really looks forward to having some company. Men or women with young children are encouraged to bring them along on weekly visits, since many older people enjoy seeing and playing with children. (Bring a few of your child's toys along.) But check first before bringing your children! Some people may only want adult company.

▶ **Hospital Visits.** They can be either once or twice a week. If the patient is going to be hospitalized over Shabbos, a Bikkur Cholim might send him flowers, grape juice, and challah on Friday.

▶ **Apartments.** The Bikkur Cholim organizations in many cities make apartments available to a patient and his family when they come to receive medical treatment. Some of these apartments are close to the hospital, while others are in the Jewish neighborhood. These apartments are maintained and ready at a moment's notice in case a family with a medical emergency needs one.

▶ **Telephone Squad.** In order for any Bikkur Cholim to be successful, there have to be volunteers willing to put in hours on the telephone, calling business owners to ask if they would be willing to donate goods or services that are needed.

One head of a Bikkur Cholim organization told me how she had wanted to apply for a grant, but simply could not find the time to gather all the information required for it. A volunteer offered to do this for her and spent an entire week on the phone getting all of the data together. As a result of her "phone duty," the organization was awarded the grant, which was used to help many families.

▶ **Group Counseling:** Many Bikkur Cholims sponsor support groups to help individuals cope with their medical problems. For instance, women who have had a mastectomy counsel other women, or couples who have undergone successful infertility treatments help guide other couples, or teenagers who have been given a clean bill of health after recovering from leukemia speak to children who are now undergoing the same treatments. These groups usually form when there is a specific need for them in the community. They provide a source of comfort for both children and adults, giving them what they need the most: hope.

Professionals and Business Owners Can Help

As discussed in the "Helping Within Your Field of Expertise" section of this chapter, offering your professional assistance or donating to the Bikkur Cholim some of the merchandise or services that your business provides can be invaluable to the people in your community. For example, an architect can help a family decide where the best place is to build a wheelchair ramp outside their home. A store owner can donate clothing, shoes, or toys, or provide them "at cost."

On the other side of the coin, people who run Bikkur Cholim organizations should keep in mind that professionals and store owners need to make a living too. Various organizations frequently solicit them to donate their time, merchandise, and (of course!) money. Naturally, these people cannot possibly remain solvent if they give away everything they have. People should not be judged if they turn down a request. Only they know what their financial situation really is, despite outward appearances.

Note: It is important to not judge the needs and wants of a family that is going through a crisis. What is a luxury for some is a necessity for others. For instance, a back massage is not just a luxury if it will ease a sick person's pain or help someone relax who has been up for nights on end nursing a sick spouse or child.

Listed below are some of the ways professionals and business owners help their local Bikkur Cholim:

▶ Merchants donate items for a monthly Shabbos package filled to the brim with things such as: fresh flowers, candies, children's books, a cake, a new game for the children to play on Shabbos. Other original ideas are: a Shabbos robe for the mother, a Shabbos tablecloth, or a nice Havdalah candle.

▶ Cleaning services donate weekly cleaning help. If a home looks chaotic, it can adversely affect the family members.

▶ Catering services or restaurants send over food from their kitchens.

▶ Wigmakers provide wigs to chemotherapy patients whose hair generally falls out after the treatments begin. Also, a new wig certainly cheers up an Orthodox woman who covers her hair and cannot afford to buy a new one because of the mounting medical expenses.

▶ Barbers donate monthly haircuts for the family.

▶ Store owners send over computer games, board games, outdoor games, roller blades — whatever is age appropriate — for the children.

▶ Beauty salons make up, or give a facial, or a manicure to women who are housebound. They also do these things for someone who is undergoing chemotherapy, so she'll feel better about going out in public. Such treatments also boost the morale of the woman who has been caring for a sick family member.

▶ Businessmen give camp scholarships to children who want to go, but the family doesn't have enough money to send them. Or they set up funds for the same purpose.

▶ Clothing merchants give families new outfits to wear before Yom Tov; even clothing from last year's inventory is appreciated. Along the same lines, they provide shoes for growing children, or hats for teenage boys.

▶ Bookstores donate whatever books the children need for school.

▶ Appliance stores donate mixers, blenders, and bread machines to those who feel too exhausted to manage routine food preparation chores.

▶ Kosher hotels donate some of their rooms to families who cannot prepare for Pesach on their own.

▶ Computer stores donate computers so that people who are housebound can e-mail their friends and family members. They can also use it as a therapeutic tool for writing down their thoughts and feelings. If the family members don't know how to use a computer, instructors donate some time to teach them the basics.

▶ Handymen and craftsmen volunteer to do some home renovations, such as installing railings alongside the staircases or lowering the kitchen cabinets to make things more accessible for a family member in a wheelchair.

▶ Medical supply stores donate wheelchairs, hospital beds, lift-out chairs, seats for washing oneself in the bathtub, walkers, etc.

▶ Businessmen donate memberships or offer substantial discounts to the local Jewish Community Center. These centers provide sports facilities for swimming, basketball, and exercise classes, as well as a place where families can get information about other Jewish agencies in town whose resources might benefit them.

Bikkur Cholims would not be able to exist, of course, without the financial support of their communities. The reason many people like to donate to Bikkur Cholim organizations is that, in most cases, 100% of the money goes to help the families in need. Usually the staff, advisory board, and people who help on a weekly or monthly basis are volunteers.

Many Bikkur Cholim organizations invite individuals to set up a fund in memory of a loved one under their auspices. They can even specify how they want the money to be used.

Chai Lifeline and Hands On for Children

If you would like to do volunteer work for an organization that deals with Jewish children who are ill, you can find out what is operating in your area from your local Bikkur Cholim chapter. Two such organizations are discussed below.

Chai Lifeline is a worldwide nonprofit organization that helps out any Jewish child who has a life-threatening illness and his/her family. Its professional staff and large corps of volunteers run a wide variety of highly acclaimed programs designed to ease the multitude of problems that these families face. Their international office is based in New York.

One of Chai Lifeline's most successful ventures is their Camp Simcha. Children who have serious medical needs that require careful monitoring can go to this kosher camp and enjoy many regular camp activities. Menucha, a counselor at Camp Simcha, described what it is like there:

> When counselors talk about Camp Simcha, we refer to the "Simcha Magic." Believe it or not, it is not a depressing place to be at all. For many ill children it is the only place where they

really feel comfortable. For a few weeks out of every year they can be in an atmosphere where they are not labeled as "the kid who has cancer" and they love that. We have so many amazing activities going on for them every day: hot air balloon rides, famous entertainers performing for them, horseback riding, outings, etc. We treat them like "real campers" and try our hardest to make Camp Simcha a "real, normal" camp.

Learning how to give to these children has changed my whole outlook on life. It has made me appreciate what I have so much more and to realize how precious life really is.

Healthy children are able to make donations to this organization, as well. Through their schools, clubs, or camps, they look for people to sponsor them for fund-raising bike-a-thons, swim-a-thons, or jumprope-a-thons. These children take their sponsorships seriously and are enthusiastic about helping such a worthy cause.

Hands On for Children is a smaller New York-based program, in which a school class "adopts" an ill child or teenager and stays in touch with him/her through letters, gifts, and home or hospital visits.

On a Personal Note: My daughter Chaya Gittel came home from a Bas Mitzvah party at her friend's house that had lasted a very long time. She said that they had worked on two crafts projects there: one which she brought home, and the other, decorating a stationery box, that would be sent to children in the Hands On for Children program. She told me that the girls really worked at trying to make the boxes especially attractive.

The next day I phoned the Bas Mitzvah girl's mother and told her what a wonderful idea I thought it was and how impressed I was with her daughter. Instead of wanting the entire party to center around her, her daughter chose to share her special day with others who were ill.

HELPING WITHIN YOUR FIELD OF EXPERTISE

If you want to help someone who is going through hard times, but you just don't know what to do, there is an incredibly simple solution for this dilemma. Help with something that you are skilled at.

When relatives and friends contact a widow and offer to advise her in any area she may be lacking knowledge in, their offer is much appreciated since, in many cases, it saves her hours and hours of research. It also saves her a great deal of anxiety and aggravation. So, if you are a stockbroker, computer consultant, school principal, lawyer, accountant, life insurance agent, doctor, or therapist, you can be of great assistance to a woman who has lost her husband.

Plumbers can teach a widow how to fix leaky faucets and toilets, mechanics can advise on how to best maintain a car, repairmen can determine whether it would be best to buy a new appliance or to fix the old one, etc. In fact, anyone who knows how to fix things around the house can be invaluable to a widow with no experience in doing such things. As we all know, there's always something around the house that could use some work!

Retired men and women can be unbelievably helpful too. They are a veritable fount of information and skills and they are happy to share what they know.

It certainly was gratifying for me and other widows I know to learn that there were people out there who cared about how we were getting along. Also, their offers to help made it much easier for us to call them back another time and ask for their opinion on whatever we needed. They made us feel that we weren't really bothering them.

It also should be noted that the person receiving help and even the person giving help might not want it known. A breach of confidentiality on either side could cause them to end their association.

As always, it is a person's prerogative to graciously refuse your help or to disagree with what you have advised him/her to do. While your help is definitely appreciated, it does not mean that the person is obligated to follow through on your suggestions.

The important thing is to set aside the time and make yourself available for someone who could use your expertise. *Kol Yisrael arevim zeh b'zeh* — All Jews are responsible for one another (*Shevuos* 39a).

Note: Many times it is assumed that widowers do not need financial advice. This is not necessarily the case, since in some households the woman takes care of the family's finances. Many times people will offer to sit down with a widow and help her set up a financial system, tell her about life insurance, and tell her what she needs to know about taxes now that she has become a single parent, but no one thinks of discussing these things with a widower. Both men and women need to know these things if they haven't been taking care of the household finances before. Also keep in mind that not every man is mechanically inclined and that some single fathers would greatly appreciate advice concerning house and car maintenance.

Example: At the time of her husband's death, Talya's two children were in college. Both she and her husband had been working in order to pay for their children's tuition at an in-state college. But without her husband's salary, Talya could no longer afford to pay their tuition.

A relative's son, Daniel, who was affiliated with a prestigious university, called Tanya up when he heard about her loss. He raised her spirits by telling her that there were ways she could keep her children in school — there were scholarships on the state and national level that she was now eligible for, since her financial situation had changed. He told her exactly where to obtain the scholarship applications and where she could find additional information. (This was thirty years before the Internet!)

As a result of Daniel's thoughtfulness, Talya was able to keep her sons in college. He also called back quite a few times afterwards to see if he could help Tanya with anything else.

Example: After Dora's husband passed away, she had no idea how she was going to file her tax return. How do you file taxes for a deceased spouse, where do you list your Social Security benefits, what forms does the government need to prove change of status — she was very nervous that she wouldn't do it right.

Then, about two months later, Dora got a call from Gila Gruenbaum, who worked in her same office complex. Gila told Dora that her husband, Stanley, was a CPA and that he would be happy to help her with all the paperwork involved in filing taxes and receiving her Social Security benefits. He had already looked into which forms she would need to fill out and what documents she would need to copy and send in.

He gave her an "assignment" and she gathered all the information he needed. When she finished, she went to the Gruenbaum's house and the three of them sat together while Stanley went over the forms with her.

To say that all of this was a tremendous help is an understatement. To this day, Stanley helps Dora with all of her tax forms and any problems with her Social Security checks.

Example: Yetta had lived on her own and had handled her own finances for years before she got married. But when she lost her husband and was responsible for all the bills plus taking care of her two young children, her old system did not work well for her.

Then, out of the blue, she got a call from an acquaintance, Shoshi, a woman whose son went to nursery school with her son. Shoshi told Yetta that she was a certified CPA and that she would be happy to help her organize her bills. Yetta decided to accept her kind offer.

The next week, Shoshi came to her house with all the supplies Yetta would need to set up her new financial system. (Yetta said that she had a good feeling about this right from the start!) Shoshi sat with her for over three hours and they accomplished an enormous amount. Yetta was able to understand her system, since Shoshi took the time to explain it practically and clearly. Ten years later, Yetta still uses the system Shoshi taught her.

Note: Please be careful, if you are helping someone to organize his/her finances, not to invade his/her privacy. The individual may not want you to learn all the details of his/her financial situation.

SHIDDUCHIM

Judaism views marriage as an intrinsic good and a source of blessing. As is written in the Torah: "It is not good for man to be alone" (Bereishis 2:18). This is where matchmaking comes in — to help others find an appropriate spouse. While this section deals mostly with matchmaking for widows and widowers, many of the suggestions can also be helpful in dealing with someone who is divorced or who has never been married.

When people are widowed, their friends and family want to see them happily married again as soon as possible. In some circumstances this is a good idea, such as when they have several young children to raise and it is very difficult for them to handle all of the responsibilities of work and children on their own. But in other cases, a waiting period is best, until they feel ready to get married again.

Some men and women begin to look into the subject as soon as the period of *Sheloshim*, the first thirty days of mourning, is over. For others, years go by before they can even entertain the thought of dating and welcoming someone else into their lives. As discussed in previous chapters, everybody has their own personal time clock, and no one should pressure a person into doing something that s/he is not ready for. Putting the past in its place and moving on to build a future with someone new is no small feat.

An individual's circumstances might be different the second time around. A widow might have children at home or even parents living with her, so she will need to consider what is in their best interest as well.

There are excellent and dedicated *shadchanim* who use whatever resources and contacts they have to find the best match available for people who turn to them. They listen to what their client has to say and they search for what he says he wants.

Unfortunately, there are also *shadchanim* who are insensitive, whose matchmaking may be motivated by a desire for money or increasing their reputations. They do not take into account many of their clients' concerns, and they do not think realistically about the future of the particular couple and the children involved.

It is a tragedy when this happens. An insensitive *shadchan* can inflict great heartache and pain on her clients by pressuring and berating them into going through with a *shidduch* that is not in his/her best interests. This is unconscionable! (A well-respected Rav, who was upset by all the divorce cases coming to him, began asking all the couples the same question: "Who was the *shadchan*?")

And even if it seems to be a good match between the man and the woman, how will it be for the children involved? It is a grave error to say, "Don't worry, everything will work out after you get married." No one should pressure a couple to go through with a marriage if they have genuine misgivings. Better to live in solitude and sanity than to enter a chaotic marriage where everyone involved is miserable and suffering. The dynamics of successfully blending two families together is quite a challenge, to say the least.

While widow/ers usually are not gullible individuals who can be easily manipulated into doing things that won't be good for them, it is important to keep in mind that loneliness can overpower them, especially after they have been half of a happily married couple for many years. Their emotions can override their logic once they grow tired of living alone. No matter what their age is, widow/ers should be encouraged to take the time to clearly and thoroughly think things through.

REMARRYING WHEN THERE ARE TEENAGERS AT HOME

There are those who think it advisable for the remaining parent to wait until his/her teenagers have completed their year of mourning before remarrying. The reason for this is that they may not be able to accept their parent's new spouse if they aren't given enough time to mourn the loss of their biological parent.

As teenagers reach a sense of closure at the end of their year of mourning, they feel like a weight has been lifted from their shoulders. While the pain of missing their parent is still there, after a year of doing things to honor that parent, their loss is put into more of a perspective. By then, they are better equipped to deal with the notion that life goes on.

This holds true not only for teenagers, but for children who are mature enough to understand their loss and need time to adjust to life without their parent. Their feelings also should be taken into consideration. What has to be kept in mind is that every family situation is unique and it makes a difference.

Before a widow/er begins dating again, s/he should consult with people who have gone through the same thing and managed to blend two families together. Children's feelings must be respected and they have to be taken into consideration before making decisions that will affect them.

Example: A friend called and told me the following:

I once went to a wedding where I met a childhood classmate of mine, Ellie, who had lost her husband and was left with three teenage children. In the course of our conversation, Ellie mentioned that she had decided not to remarry until her children were out of the house and on their own. She felt it would be too difficult to patch together two families; and also, Ellie added, she wanted to raise her children in a certain way and did not want to have to compromise on that.

I didn't say anything at the time, but I thought to myself that such a young woman would be better off remarried than alone. Truthfully, I thought that Ellie was being ridiculous!

But now that I have lost my husband and remarried, I understand what Ellie was talking about. Remarrying is much harder than anyone thinks. When I did it, my husband and I had half a dozen children (ages 5–16) between us, and there were some major adjustments both sides had to go through. If my husband had not been so patient and understanding about our situation these past few years, I do not know if I could have stuck it out myself!

And to think that I had to become a widow before I could respect Ellie's decision. She really knew what she was talking about; she just had reached a different conclusion than I had, based on her and her children's needs. It was a tough decision for her to make since it's hard to raise children alone. I have the utmost admiration and respect for her.

On a Personal Note: Some say that the hardest loss of all is to lose a child, because it is not the way of the world for a child to die before his parent. With this in mind, I would like to praise those special parents who have lost an adult son or daughter and then generously encouraged their son-in-law or daughter-in-law to remarry.

While researching this book I heard many stories about parents who were able to think of what was best for their son-in-law or daughter-in-law and grandchildren — in spite of their crushing grief. They were the ones who tactfully encouraged the widow/er to move on with his/her life and live it to the fullest.

Not only that, but once their son- or daughter-in-law remarried, these parents treated the new spouse's children as their own grandchildren. These parents deserve the highest accolades for selflessness and concern for others. They bestow peace and well-being to their family in spite of their personal pain and loss.

Example: Sylvia and Steve Collins tragically lost their daughter, a young mother of two small children, several years ago. Their son-in-law remarried after a few years and the Collinses remained very much a part of their grandchildren's lives.

Recently they announced the happy news that their new "daughter-in-law" was expecting. Both parents said they were thrilled to know that the couple was going to have children of their own, too, and they felt as happy as if the new wife were their own daughter! What exceptional human beings they are!

The following are some do's and don'ts for making a good *shidduch*. When you are considerate of others, your efforts will be appreciated.

▶ **Find out the Hebrew names of the single people you know and make sure to pray for them daily.** It is considered especially good to do this when you light Shabbos candles. Once you become engaged, married, and during your first year of marriage, try to show your gratitude for finding your special partner by praying for someone who hasn't found his or hers yet.

▶ **Keep an index card file in your home that separately lists all the single males and females you know or have heard about.** Look it over whenever you add a new name to see if anyone there is appropriate for the new addition. Jot down specific details that are important, such as: age, Jewish education and level of observance, marital history, profession, personality, and what the person is looking for.

▶ **Keep your friends in mind if you are single and you have dated a lovely person who simply wasn't right for you — but may be for one of them.** And do not forget your single friends once you have married or remarried. Your new spouse may have a friend who is suitable for someone you know. (But please don't invite unsuspecting guests for surprise introductions at your Shabbos table. This can create a very uncomfortable situation.) Also, do not get insulted if a person refuses a *shidduch* you suggest. People have valid reasons for doing so and it definitely should not deter you from trying to find someone else for them at another time.

▶ **Arrange the *shidduch* even if you do not have time to act as the go-between in clarifying details and working out issues.** Just tell them both from the beginning and, if you can, help them find someone else they feel comfortable with who can serve that purpose. Your family obligations come first, but you still will have done a good thing by making the match.

If you do not know someone well, she will take it as a compliment that you bothered to call her up to ask her about herself and what she is looking for. Whether you are a parent of child's friend in school, or share a car pool with her, or have met her at a *simchah*, or haven't spoken to her in years, it is certainly appropriate for you to inquire about her either directly or through a close friend. (But be considerate enough not to have this discussion in a public place!)

▶ **It is cruel to mention a *shidduch* to someone and then never bring it up again.** It is also very rude to call someone and ask for all his personal details and then never call back. If the other party does not want to go out with this person, do the courteous thing and let him know. Tell the person that you will keep him in mind if something else comes up.

▶ **Learn the laws of *lashon ha-ra* as they apply to *shidduchim*.** The subject of guarding our speech is extremely important! You will be amazed to learn what you are required to tell and what you should not mention. A qualified Rabbi or lecturer on the topic of *lashon ha-ra* will be able to answer your questions and direct you to the best book to study. Do not take this issue lightly. Many divorces could have been prevented if only the right questions were asked and answered honestly before the wedding. You are not helping anyone by not telling the whole truth. Speak to a qualified person to determine if a particular issue you know about eventually could be detrimental to the marriage.

There are classes, seminars, and Shabbatonim for those who want to become more knowledgeable about how to make matches. Also, there are organizations and certain *shadchanim* dedicated to the cause of making good, successful second marriages. If you want to make a *shidduch*, try to find out how the person is most comfortable being approached. Bring up the subject diplomatically and convey how much you care for the person's welfare so that you do not appear to be prying into their personal business.

On a Personal Note: One woman told me that she was recently asked, "Why did it take you fifteen years to remarry after your husband died?" She responded, "It was the only good *shidduch* offered to me in all those years!"

Unfortunately, that seems to be true of many widows today. And yet, there are still some exceptional men who are willing to go that extra mile to marry into a family where they will have the challenge (and honor!) of being some child's father. These men are held in great esteem since it is more in the nature of a woman than a man to take on someone else's children and raise and treat them as her own. Men can become wonderful stepfathers, if only they are given the chance to meet the right woman and her children. Introducing them to each other is a great mitzvah.

Chapter Six

Things You Can Do to Help on the Sabbath and the Festivals

Being a religious Jew, my life re-
volves around all the Sabbaths and
Festivals throughout the Jewish calen-
dar. The hectic pace of my daily life does
not provide me with much of an opportunity
to stop and contemplate my circumstances. Yet,
in the calming atmosphere of Shabbos and Yom Tov I find enough
time to relax and reflect. It is then that my memories and my sup-
pressed emotions always seem to surface. These are the times when
I miss Dovid the most. I imagine it is the same for anyone who has
lost a loved one.

Shabbos and Yom Tov present a huge challenge to widow/ers,
especially if they have children living at home and must assume the
roles of both parents. They have to get used to doing all the things
they never had to do before in a limited amount of time. Sometimes
the holiday requires doing something that is gender-specific that
they cannot take care of personally.

This chapter describes all the different ways that people can
help make Shabbos and Yom Tov a happier and more relaxed time
for those who have lost a family member. Many of these stories are
personal accounts — mine and those I gathered from the interviews
I conducted.

SHABBOS AND YOM TOV IN GENERAL

Shabbos and Yom Tov were meant to bring peace and joy into the hearts of the Jewish People. Yet, when one's heart is full of sorrow after the loss of a loved one, it is hard to feel these things. Shabbos and Yom Tov then become both lonely and trying times — emotionally, physically, or both.

For a widow or a widower, Shabbos and the Festivals take on a bittersweet taste once they have to do all the things that their husband or wife used to do. For a father it means lighting the Shabbos/Yom Tov candles, making sure that all the food and clothing preparations are done, cleaning the house, etc. For a mother it means reciting *Kiddush, HaMotzi,* and Havdalah, finding someone to take her sons to shul, leading discussions about the weekly Torah portion at the table, etc.

It is an enormous job to be both the mother and father every Shabbos and Yom Tov, especially the first year after a spouse passes away. Many widows I spoke with told me about various "tricks" they relied on to help get them through the day(s). They bought music tapes to play on Fridays or *erev Yom Tov,* baked and (miraculously!) hid a special dessert that they knew their kids really liked, or saved a particular magazine or book just for that day. Before a Festival, they would treat themselves to something new: a scarf, a dress, a robe, etc. It is remarkable what looking forward to something special can do for one's whole state of mind!

In the beginning, these women found it particularly difficult to maintain proper decorum at the Shabbos table in the dining room while, at the same time, supervising what went on in the kitchen. For example, listening to one child tell a story from the weekly Torah portion while at the same time making sure that the other children helping in the kitchen didn't spill hot soup onto themselves was very trying! But they were able to make things more manageable by cutting down on the number of courses in the meal and simplifying things in other ways.

If they ventured out with their "whole gang" for a Shabbos meal, they chose homes that had a relaxed atmosphere so they could enjoy themselves without worrying every time their children were a bit noisy or rambunctious. Occasionally they invited families over for a Shabbos meal, but only families they were especially close to. They knew that those husbands would not feel uncomfortable about assuming the male role at their Shabbos table, and this, naturally, took a great burden off them.

Another thing they did for Shabbos was to invite a few of their single friends over. They helped just by telling *parashah* stories or singing songs with the children so that their mother could get the food ready in the kitchen. The children really enjoyed the exclusive attention lavished on them from these special Shabbos guests. It was a very good solution for long, cold winter Friday nights, instead of struggling to get the children into their coats, boots, and gloves to go out somewhere.

Even though everyone felt that an "important person" was missing at the Shabbos table, having guests helped pull the family together. It was also important for the children to see that guests liked coming over and felt comfortable in their home.

Note: If there are teenagers in the family, they might not be as receptive as younger children are to eating at other families' homes where they do not feel comfortable. They might agree to socialize only with a few select families, or they might prefer to invite a close friend of theirs over to join them for the meal while the rest of the family goes out. It all depends on the individual. But, it is extremely important to be considerate of their feelings, because they are experiencing the loss and the change, too.

On a Personal Note: One *erev Shabbos*, a few months after Dovid passed away, my daughter asked me why I never played Tatti's music tapes on Friday afternoons anymore. Although I didn't particularly want to be reminded of our life "before," I found them and played them to make her happy.

The funny thing was that the familiar getting-ready-for-Shabbos music made me feel happy, too! It had a quieting effect on my nerves as I rushed around trying to get everything done. I felt that — even though Dovid wasn't going to walk through the door at any minute — he was still watching over us and our Shabbos preparations. From that week on I played those tapes on *erev Shabbos* the minute my children came home from school.

When planning your Shabbos or Yom Tov meals, try to think of the people who might be eating alone and ask yourself if it is at all possible to have a single guest or a single-parent family over. People feel good when they know that they have a place to go for Shabbos and Yom Tov. Try to invite them several days in advance so that they don't feel like an "afterthought" that you only got around to calling the night before.

Individuals and families are not comfortable in every social setting. One single woman mentioned that she prefers to be the only guest when she is invited out; she doesn't like to "be bunched together with all of the other single people in town." Yet, another single woman feels more comfortable when there are other singles or families present. A widow with teenagers said that her children enjoy going to people whom they know for Shabbos, but feel extremely uncomfortable if any other families are there. (The reason for this is that her teenage son makes *Kiddush* for them, and he feels very self-conscious doing this in front of people he does not know.)

So, when extending an invitation, be sure to mention what other guests you are inviting for the meal. That way, the person can either accept or refuse your invitation and there won't be any unpleasant surprises later. Don't just assume that people won't mind. Also, don't put a person on the spot and ask why he is turning down your invitation. Just tell the person that you will call back another time, and be sure to follow through.

There are, of course, times when you will get a last-minute phone call from a single person who needs a place for Shabbos. If you know that your already invited company will not feel comfortable with this person (or vice-versa), it is perfectly acceptable to say that you are already booked. Perhaps you can help him figure out whom else to call.

There are, of course, other valid reasons for not having company, such as: you already have a lot of guests; your family needs some quiet, quality time together; your family is just getting over the flu; you and your husband have major problems and the tension is evident; you have had an unusually hard week; you are taking care of an ailing family member. All of these reasons are legitimate and you should not feel guilty. In fact, it is preferable not to invite guests over if any one of the above is the case!

Making guests feel like a part of your family by inviting them often for Shabbos and/or Yom Tov is one of the most considerate things you can do. Yes, it may inconvenience you a bit, but who says you have to prepare an elaborate meal? Throw a few extra potatoes in the cholent, serve fruit for dessert instead of a fancy concoction, or buy the challahs that week instead of baking them yourself. You have no idea how good it makes a person feel to know that he has a place to go for Shabbos or Yom Tov!

On Another Personal Note: We live in a community that took us in with open arms, and, thank God, Shabbos and Yom

Tov invitations were plentiful. Thank you to my wonderful friends and neighbors in Baltimore.

Example: A young mother passed away, leaving her husband with two small daughters. Harriet, one of the neighbors on their block, saw that the widower was being inundated with Shabbos invitations. She felt that the family needed more continuity in order to establish a normal Shabbos routine. Knowing that her husband got along very well with this young father, Harriet invited him to come every week for the Friday night Shabbos meal and he happily accepted her offer. This family became regular guests for years, no matter what the weather was outside. In fact, these two families became so close that Harriet attended all the mother-daughter activities at the girls' school.

Harriet feels that by "adopting" this family, her teenage children gained new respect for their parents and a greater appreciation for their own family. She commented that now that her children are married, she sees that they are very devoted to inviting guests over for Shabbos in their own homes.

On a Personal Note: Before the holidays, think of those who are alone or going through hard times (i.e., someone who has lost a close relative or friend, someone who is divorced or who never married, a childless couple, a disabled person, an *agunah*, a family with someone who has a life-threatening illness, etc.) and call to wish them a "Good Yom Tov." Or, send these people a card to let them know you are thinking of them, or invite them for a meal, or buy them a book you think they would like, or bake them a special treat, or send them flowers. These little things mean the world to them!

It is a custom in some families for the husbands to give their wives a gift of jewelry before a Festival. This is certainly not a Jewish law, but rather a nice way for the husband to show his wife how much he appreciates her hard work. There have been times when a widow's children, family members, or friends got together and bought her a small piece of jewelry before the Festivals to keep up her husband's custom. This is a most touching and thoughtful gesture, especially during the first year after the husband died. (It should be noted that a gift of jewelry does not have to be very expensive.)

HAVDALAH

At the close of Shabbos or Yom Tov, when it is time to hear Havdalah, many singles and single parents with children are invited to friends or relatives who live in their building or on their block. Some halachic authorities say that, if at all possible, one should try to hear Havdalah from a Jewish male over the age of Bar Mitzvah.

On a Personal Note: The first week we were all together for Shabbos in Baltimore after Dovid passed away, there was a knock on our front door around Havdalah time. I answered the door and there stood one of the neighborhood boys, Gedalya Rosen. Gedalya had come over (of his own volition, his mother later told me) to make Havdalah for us. I was so pleased — and so were my children! He did this every week that he was home from yeshiva until we moved away from that particular block.

ROSH HASHANAH

Rosh Hashanah and the other High Holidays that follow present tactical problems that require some planning. On Rosh Hashanah, everyone must attend synagogue during the day and hear the shofar being blown. Many synagogues arrange a special shofar blowing after the morning services to make it more convenient for the mothers of young children to fulfill this mitzvah. Women arrive after the *Shacharis* service, hand their children over to their husbands to watch, and go in to hear the shofar. But what is a widow going to do with her children?

What some women do to help one another is take turns watching each other's children at home. (This arrangement not only enables the woman to hear the shofar, but it also gives her some time to pray in shul.) It also provides a much calmer alternative to taking little children to synagogue and anxiously hoping that some kind person will offer to watch them while their mother goes to hear the shofar!

Example: One of Suri's children had a bad case of the flu. She didn't want to take him out since he wasn't feeling well, but she couldn't ask anyone to watch him while she went out, because he was contagious. She concluded that she just would not be able to hear the shofar blowing that day.

In the early afternoon, there was a knock at Suri's door. A neighbor had heard about her predicament and had sent her husband over to blow the shofar for her!

In Orthodox synagogues, men and women sit separately. It is a very thoughtful gesture to call a single parent and offer to sit with his/her children and help them with their prayers. If a mother has to stay home with her younger children, she will surely appreciate someone supervising her sons in shul. I have also heard of a case in which a father asked a woman to sit next to his teenage daughters during the services.

Example: A young, recently divorced woman wanted someone to sit with her young boys in shul. She called the Rav of her congregation to ask who he thought would not mind doing this.

"I know just the right man for the job!" he assured her. "Tell your boys to come to me when they get to shul and I'll introduce them."

On Rosh Hashanah, this woman sent her boys off to find the Rav and she went to say her prayers in the women's section. When it was time for her to leave, she peeked into the men's section to see if she could find her boys, and there they were, sitting in front of the entire congregation on either side of the Rav — with huge smiles on their faces!

Note: While women are obligated to go to the synagogue a few times a year, men are obligated to pray with a *minyan* (with at least nine other men) every day. This presents quite a challenge for a single father of small children. Any time you can watch his children so that he can get to the synagogue would be very helpful. When the need arose in my town, my daughters joined a rotating group of teenagers who took care of a widower's children on Shabbos mornings once a month.

Example: A widower once mentioned how his wonderful neighbor always included his little girls in shopping for holiday clothes whenever she took her own daughters. He said this neighbor lifted an enormous weight from his shoulders every time she did this.

On a Personal Note: My mother's closest friend, Shirley Shulman, used to bake small, absolutely delicious honey cakes before Rosh Hashanah and give them to everyone who was living alone in our small Jewish community. When I got married, I decided to continue Aunt Shirley's honey cake tradition in her memory. I told my children to give them to our neighbors who were not religious, to remind them of the upcoming holidays and to wish them a good year.

After Dovid died, I decided to bake a few extra honey cakes for my friends who were single, divorced, or widowed. I piled all the kids into the car to make these other deliveries.

From the back seat, one of my daughters asked why we were giving these cakes to just a few people and not to all of our friends, like on Purim. I explained that at this time of year, around the holidays, it is nice to remember people who are alone — to reach out and try to make their holiday happier by letting them know that we are thinking of them.

After we made all of our deliveries, we returned home... and there on my porch was a magnificent bouquet of flowers from a good friend, with a card attached wishing me a "Good Yom Tov." (I must add here that when my youngest son saw the bouquet, he asked, "Mommy, why is someone sending flowers to YOU?")

Example: Zilpah said that for the past three years since her husband died, she has received more phone calls than usual beginning with the month of Elul and continuing through Sukkos. The callers are friends or family members who live as far away as Israel or England. Even if the calls come from just around the corner, she appreciates them all because "it's just so nice to be remembered with a phone call before Yom Tov!"

YOM KIPPUR

Yom Kippur is an intense, physically demanding day in two-parent households. Now try to imagine what it is like for one parent to juggle all of the family responsibilities while fasting. If it can be arranged, single parents of little children would also like to spend some time in synagogue concentrating on the spiritual aspect of the day and not only on their children's physical needs.

Yizkor is a memorial prayer recited for the departed members of one's immediate family on Shemini Atzeres, the last day of Pesach, Shavuos and, as is more widely known, on Yom Kippur. Children should recite Yizkor once they reach the age of Bar or Bas Mitzvah, but they can say it when they are younger if they want to.

Complications arise when the children want to say *Yizkor* for a parent or sibling and there is not a parent who can stand beside them. (It is a custom that congregants whose parents are living leave the synagogue for the few minutes that the *Yizkor* prayer is said.) Young children can feel intimidated standing alone, because the room is usually filled with adults, who may stare at them curiously. Eventually, the children get used to it and the adults get used to them being there. Curious people should exercise some self-control so that they don't make the situation even more difficult for these children. It is helpful if a relative or good friend can stand with the children.

Example: When *Yizkor* was announced one Yom Kippur, a widowed friend's daughters remained in the women's section, while my friend left because both her parents were still living. A woman, who saw that the little girls had stayed, promptly marched over to them and said in a loud whisper, "You girls don't belong here! Go out right now!"

Her girls were really shaken up, but the older one had the wits to reply, "We have to say *Yizkor* for our father." The woman was greatly embarrassed and apologized immediately, but that did not ease the emotional pain she had caused.

On a Personal Note: My oldest daughter Raizel, at the tender age of eight, a year after my husband passed away, asked me on Yom Kippur morning, "Mommy, aren't I suppose to go to shul and say a prayer for Tatti today?" So that started my children's tradition of reciting *Yizkor* for their father in shul beginning from the age of eight.

On Another Personal Note: Since Dovid died, Ita and Yoni Hershkowitz have become a big part of our lives. So much so that my kids call them "Aunt" and "Uncle," and they treat my children like their own. On *erev Yom Kippur* there is a custom to recite a special blessing over one's children. And so, after Yoni gives his own children a *berachah* (blessing), he comes over to our house to give my children a *berachah*, too.

When he walks in the door, one of my kids announces, "Uncle Yoni is here!" From the oldest to the youngest they line up in front of him and he blesses them — with his eyes closed, intent on what he is saying. It is a very emotional time. After he finishes, he nods to me and heads back to his house. (I also bless my children on *erev Yom Kippur*, but those extra *berachos* for my family are greatly appreciated.)

SUKKOS

After Yom Kippur, many families sit down to break their fast, and as soon as the meal is over, they are up again building their *sukkos* in preparation for the next holiday. If you live in a religious neighborhood you will hear the loud banging of hammers late into the night. Below are some suggestions of how you can help someone else with the mitzvos and traditions of Sukkos:

▶ A teenager or an adult can volunteer to help a family that has lost a husband, father, or son, with putting up and taking down their *sukkah*.

▶ If you know of a family that spends Sukkos out of town with relatives because one of the parents is deceased, ask the children in that family to help you and your children put up your *sukkah* or ask them to help decorate your *sukkah*. Everyone in school will be talking about what they did to get ready for Sukkos, and these children will otherwise feel left out.

Example: Every Sukkos a widow's married children, who live out of town, come to spend the holiday with her. However, their jobs keep them from arriving at her house until *erev Sukkos*. Knowing this, every year her neighbors build her *sukkah* before they build their own.

Example: A widow with three boys in elementary school would take them to her parents' home every Sukkos. However, she always made arrangements for her young sons to help their friends' fathers put up their *sukkos*. This way, her children did not feel left out when their classmates talked about how they were helping to put up their *sukkos*. And when they went to their grandparents' home, they brought along all of the Sukkos decorations they had made in school and hung them up in the *sukkah* there. This really made them feel that they had participated in getting ready for the Festival like everyone else.

▶ If a family does not have a father, try to include the sons when you purchase items boys need for the holiday.

Example: Every year a close friend of the family comes with his two sons to help a widow and her young teenage boys put up their *sukkah* and take it down again a week later. This man also takes her sons along with him and his sons when they go to buy their set of Four Species and the *sechach* for covering the *sukkah*. He thus helps them make their selections, and being with others increases their pre-holiday spirits.

▶ Try to make room for those who would definitely appreciate joining you for a meal.

▶ Try to accept an invitation from a single-parent family to join them for a meal. After putting up their *sukkah* and decorating it, the children will want to show off their artistry. Taking the time to beautify a *sukkah* and then having to eat alone in it can ruin a family's holiday. The most beautiful *sukkah* decoration of all is family and friends eating together in the *sukkah* during the holiday.

▶ Include those who would benefit from your companionship during *Chol Ha-Moed* (the intermediate days of Sukkos and Pesach) plans as well.

Example: The first Sukkos after Leib Schacter lost his wife was a pretty bleak time for him and his two teenage sons. Leib said that what helped him to get through those hard days were the many invitations that he and his sons received to eat in friends' *sukkos*. And they also enjoyed the all-day hiking trip they went on with their neighbors, the Goldsteins (they took a portable *sukkah* along with them). Leib said that the trip was especially enjoyable for him because it was the first time in a long time that he had seen both of his sons look happy.

On a Personal Note: On the block where Dovid and I purchased our first home, we had many Jewish neighbors who were not religious. We made a conscious effort to invite them to our *sukkah* for a meal. One neighbor told us, "I have lived to be in my 70s and this is the first time that I am eating in a *sukkah*." Another couple we invited enjoyed it so much that they built their own *sukkah* the following year.

I believe that having those guests is the reason why my children and I were blessed with receiving so many invitations for meals at other people's houses after we lost Dovid. There really is a domino effect in life: the *chesed* that goes around comes around. And it certainly did in my case.

On Another Personal Note: We always spent Sukkos with my brother and sister-in-law, Harris and Hadar Bram in the years after Dovid died. Although I was happy to be there, I just couldn't sit still in the *sukkah* the first night. I felt overcome by emotion seeing all the *sukkah* decorations our children had made and knowing that Dovid wasn't with me to share the *nachas*. I kept jumping up, either to serve everyone or to clear the table at every course.

Hadar and I devised a plan to help me. After the table was set in the *sukkah*, and the kids were bathed and dressed and playing quietly downstairs, she would ask me, "Are you ready?" Then we would go up to her bedroom and sit down on her bed and... cry! We cried and cried until I was pretty sure I didn't have one tear left! Then, after washing our faces, we would put on our make-up and go back downstairs. The crying afforded me a great deal of relief and the children felt more relaxed because I was actually able to remain seated during the meal.

SIMCHAS TORAH

While most men are joyfully dancing in the synagogue with their children on Simchas Torah, those who are childless, or who have lost a child, as well as children who have lost their fathers, feel awkward. Who should they dance with? How can they repress their feelings of sadness in this very public setting?

Example: Menashe was a man in his late thirties who had been married for over eight years. He and his wife were childless, but very hopeful. They were active in a Jewish Infertility Support Group in their town, where couples shared information in order to help one another. They went to the best doctor in town who specialized in infertility problems and followed his instructions very carefully, and, as Menashe would tell people, his wife had memorized many chapters of *Tehillim* in the course of praying for Hashem to bless them with a child.

One Simchas Torah, after the many lively rounds of dancing with the Torah had ended, Menashe sat down to listen to the Torah reading in the synagogue. He was tired from all the singing and dancing — he had even danced with many of his friends' children on his shoulders. He was trying to keep his spirits up, even though he felt very sad that he did not have a child of his own there. He was also fighting his disappointment — he and his wife had thought that she was finally expecting, but then they had learned the day before that she was not pregnant after all.

While sitting there quietly, listening to the Torah reading and absorbed in his own thoughts, the Rabbi's small son came and sat down next to him. Menashe was very friendly with this child, since he and his wife had been to the rabbi's house several times for Shabbos meals. When this little boy gave him a glowing smile, Menashe suddenly began to cry. He could not manage to hold his sadness in any longer. And, just then, he was called up to the Torah for an *aliyah*.

Menashe was terribly embarrassed, but he couldn't stop crying. He walked over to the *bimah* despite his tears and noticed the hushed silence all around him. He figured that everyone had probably guessed what his tears were about and that was why everyone had suddenly become quiet.

Menashe believed that his heartfelt prayers and tears of anguish, joined with the silent prayers of everyone else in the congregation, had a great deal to do with the wonderful news that he and his wife received just a few months later. His wife gave birth to a beautiful baby girl a few weeks after Simchas Torah the following year.

In retrospect, Menashe explained that his wife's friends had been very considerate of her feelings and sensitive to her needs all those years while she was childless. But, being a man, he had not found a way to express his own pain to his friends.

CHANUKAH

Since Chanukah is such a child-oriented holiday, parents try to create as happy an atmosphere as they can. Yet, Chanukah nights are very hard for a family the first few years after the father dies. For eight nights the children peer out of their living room window and see the neighbors' children eagerly peering through theirs, waiting for their fathers to come home and light the menorah. In a single-parent home, however, they simply check their Jewish calendars to know what time to light. They wait for no one's arrival.

The following are ways in which you can lend a hand and help raise such a family's spirits on Chanukah:

Teenagers can bake the traditional Chanukah sugar cookies with young children. They may just use a cookie cutter to stamp holiday-related shapes in the cookie dough or they can decorate the cookies, too.

Example: Malky said, "When my children were younger, our different helpers would come to bake. I supplied all of the ingredients and then the children would ban me from the kitchen while the kids made cookie menorahs, stars of David, or Maccabees. They liked to surprise me with the way they decorated their cookies. Then we saved them for a very special treat to have on Shabbos Chanukah."

*   *   *

Invite anyone who would benefit from your company for a Chanukah meal. On the other hand, if a family has a sick person at home who has difficulty going out, it might be easier for friends and other family members to go there to visit or for a meal. Try to make every effort to go to a housebound family like this, if at all possible. They too are deserving of having a festive atmosphere in their home.

Example: In the Feldbaum family, Chanukah is just not Chanukah without going one night to our good friends, Ora and Mendel Wolf. My kids really look forward to this because they enjoy the Wolfs' festive Chanukah atmosphere. They also look forward to having a rousing game of Spin the Dreidel!

*   *   *

Chanukah treats and gifts are most appreciated in a situation where the family members can neither go out nor even entertain company. If you know of a family in this situation, you can bring them a batch of your Chanukah cookies, or make them a special latke meal, or buy balloons or small, affordable presents for the children, etc. Once you get your children involved in this project, your whole Chanukah atmosphere will be much brighter, too!

On a Personal Note: I knew that our first Chanukah without Dovid would be really hard, so I made arrangements for us to visit friends on most of the Chanukah nights. But, as it turned out, two of my kids came down with the chicken pox, so we ended up staying home.

Friends' phone calls and quick visits during the week really helped, but two acquaintances who came over really saved the day. Aidel Newman brought balloons for everyone. One balloon even had a head and feet and hands on it; my kids danced with that one for hours. Shulamis Wiener brought an enormous paint kit and my kids got hours of fun out of that. These two women, who I barely knew, just wanted to do something to reach out to me. To this day I appreciate their compassion and warmth. It helped make the kids' (and my) Chanukah brighter.

On Another Personal Note: Even after making Chanukah a fun-filled holiday for my children, I still get choked up on the last night, looking at all the flames blazing away in our menorahs. But then one of the themes of Chanukah always comes to mind — that in the midst of the darkness (hard times) there is always a ray of light (hope).

PURIM

Purim, like Chanukah, is definitely a child-oriented holiday! On Purim, many mitzvos must be done within a twenty-four hour period. Although it is a happy holiday, attending to all of the things that need to be taken care of before and during Purim can place a lot of pressure on a single parent with young children, and be overwhelming for anyone who recently lost a loved one.

Below are a few things you can do to help:

▶ **Make *shalach manos* with the children.** Just like children love to make and decorate Chanukah cookies, they enjoy making hamentashen, too. You can also put together and decorate the *shalach manos* food packages with them.

▶ **Costumes.** I think that each child's costume is the most important thing to him on Purim. However, a good costume requires either sewing or buying, and this could be beyond a single father's capability or might require too much time or money for a single mother. If sewing is your forte, you can be very helpful to a family in this way — especially if they have a lot of children.

On a Personal Note: The year Dovid died, Zlata Kahn, a friend of mine who is a wonderful seamstress, called to tell me I could borrow costumes for my younger boys from the outgrown costumes she had made for her sons. Another friend, Rochelle Neiman, took my girls with her daughters to a used clothing shop to hunt for garments that would make good Purim costumes. They got beautiful Queen Esther and gypsy-style outfits very cheaply. Rochelle cut off the bottom of the long gowns, hemmed them on her sewing machine, and made my two daughters very, very happy! My friends were aware of my non-existent sewing abilities and I appreciated their help very much.

▶ **Hearing the Megillah.** We to go synagogue to hear the Megillah reading twice on Purim — once at night and once in the morning — and we are required to hear every single word. Therefore it would be inappropriate to bring young children along. Hiring a babysitter or special helpers ahead of time is no easy task, since there are so many activities going on during Purim, and teenagers don't want to miss any of it. A teenager who volunteers to help out a single parent in this way is a real lifesaver!

On a Personal Note: The first year after Dovid died, I didn't think I could deal with the commotion in synagogue. Rivka and Simcha Greenberg, close friends of mine, took all of my children along with theirs to hear the Megillah. I then was able to go to a private Megillah reading in someone's home. I was so grateful not to have to face a lot of people that Purim, and I certainly didn't want to dampen my children's Purim spirit. The Greenbergs' kind offer took into consideration both what was good for my children and for me.

▶ **Delivering** *Shalach Manos.* If you live in a large Jewish community, it is a big challenge to deliver *shalach manos* to everyone's teachers, friends, family members, neighbors, etc., even in two-parent homes. A teenager with kindhearted parents and an extra hour or two to spare can make a tremendous difference by helping with some of these deliveries!

On a Personal Note: Throughout the years, various teenage girls have taken my children along with them to make some of the *shalach manos* deliveries I couldn't get to. For example, one year one of my children had the flu and I could not leave the house to make my own deliveries. Some teenagers were delivering *shalach manos* for an organization, and they offered to take my kids along to help them while dropping off our *shalach manos* packages, too.

▶ **Purim Seudah.** People look forward to a festive Purim *seudah* weeks in advance. Invite a person or a family who needs cheering up to your Purim meal.

Example: The year after Dovid died, Elisheva and Yehuda Sherman invited us to their *seudah*. Afterwards, I had a lot of trouble getting my four sugar-laden kids back home and into bed. In the years that followed, the Shermans agreed to join us at our home for the *seudah*. My children liked the idea of hosting others in our home because we go away for Pesach and Sukkos.

On Another Personal Note: I would like to stress that it is not what you put in your *shalach manos* that is so important, but rather whom you send them to. Purim provides an opportunity for parents to teach their children the importance of giving — not just to their regular friends but also to those who they know will not receive a lot of packages. A shy classmate, a new child in town, someone with a disability, someone whose family has recently suffered a loss, etc. — these are the children who will appreciate *shalach manos* the most! If you know of such a child, make his Purim special by giving him his own special package. Seeing you do acts of kindness definitely has a positive effect on your children! One Purim my youngest child carefully made a special *shalach manos* package for one of his friends who was recently diagnosed with diabetes.

Example: One mother told me about her daughter Anne. "The problem is that Anne looks like any other child, but she has severe learning disabilities. She is really a very sweet girl, but once you are around her for more than a few minutes it is obvious that her IQ is below normal. She goes to a special school, but she still has to interact with the neighborhood children.

"I spoke to many of the parents on our block about how their children were teasing Anne and making her feel bad, but they just shrugged their shoulders as if to say, 'Well, kids will be kids.'

"Then a wonderful thing happened! A new family moved into the largest house on our street. Children from blocks around loved to play at that house because it had the biggest backyard and an enormous swing set. When the mother noticed how the neighborhood children were tormenting Anne, she made it clear that anyone who made fun of her or did not let her play with them was not welcome at her home. This special woman changed the attitude of all these children. They became more accepting of Anne and eventually the majority of them began to play with her on their own.

"That year, Anne received more *shalach manos* packages from the neighborhood kids than any of my other children. Her eyes were so full of joy and happiness that Purim — and mine were filled with tears."

On Another Personal Note: The first Purim without Dovid was pretty bleak, to say the least! I tried to keep everyone's spirits up, but at the same time I was feeling overwhelmed by all of the things that needed arranging, i.e., preparing the costumes, baking the hamentaschen, hearing the Megillah twice, preparing the *shalach manos* packages, delivering them, etc. I felt like I was being tossed around inside a dryer!

In the middle of the afternoon the doorbell rang. I opened it and to my astonishment there stood two clowns! One of them was carrying a boom box and the other one was holding some balloons. I just stood there with my mouth open in surprise and they gestured for me to let them in. Some of the neighborhood kids who had seen them get out of their car followed them into our house, too. The clowns plugged in their boom box and began dancing enthusiastically in a circle to the Jewish music. My kids were so excited! There were clowns dancing right in the middle of their living room! Most of the kids joined in and the clowns gave them candy and blew up more balloons. They added such *simchah* to our house!

The clowns didn't say one single word — they just made hand gestures. They stayed for about ten minutes, and then as quickly as they came, they left! We had no idea who they were.

The next year the clowns came back and all the kids on the block came to see them. This time I had my wits about me and I offered them some Purim *gelt*, telling them how much joy they had added to our holiday — but they refused to take any money. Instead, they kept giving out candies and dancing to the blasting music.

The clowns have since returned every Purim and now my kids don't want to go with me to deliver the *shalach manos* for fear that they will miss seeing them! This past year the clowns didn't even make it into our house! My sons and some of the neighborhood kids were waiting for them on our front porch, so they set up their boom box on our front lawn and started dancing with everyone. Believe me, we stopped traffic both ways! I did a little investigating and my sources told me that the clowns do it for *tzedakah* (charity). Some very thoughtful person in the community sponsors their visits to those homes that need a little extra cheer on Purim.

PESACH

The weeks before Pesach are so stressful for most women that there is even a joke about it: Two non-Jewish women decide that their religion makes no sense and they become interested in Judaism. They go to the rabbis and ask them to teach them all that they need to know so that they can convert. They beg and plead and finally, after about two years, the rabbis give in and start teaching them. Once they complete their studies, they start begging and pleading with the rabbis again to perform the conversion. Finally, after about another two years, the rabbis finally agree to allow them to convert. The women are overjoyed. "Oh thank you, rabbis!" they cry. "But can we just wait until after Pesach?"

The stress of preparing for Pesach takes on a whole new meaning for a family with a critically ill person at home, or a family who has just suffered the loss of a loved one. But how can a person find time to help out others during this exceptionally busy time of year? Despite the pressures, there are many ways that you can find some time to help people in such a difficult situation:

▶ When you are going to the grocery store, call and ask if they need anything.

▶ Invite their to children come over to play when your children are at home, so they can keep each other entertained.

▶ If you have teenagers at home and you can spare them for a while, send them over to babysit or to help with the Pesach cleaning. Teenage boys can carry heavy boxes of Pesach dishes and pots up from the basement or wherever they are stored.

▶ Invite them over for a take-out or home-cooked pre-Pesach meal.

▶ Call and ask them how their cleaning is coming along or go over and visit and give your friend a big, reassuring hug.

Example: Avital's husband passed away right before Pesach. When the week of *Shivah* was over, she didn't know how she would manage to get ready for Pesach with her young children underfoot. Fortunately, a group of teenagers volunteered to clean her entire house! The teenage boys spent a few days cleaning her basement and some of the bedrooms and bringing up the boxes of Pesach dishes and pots and pans, and carrying down the dishes they used during the rest of the year. When the boys completed their assigned jobs, the teenage girls came the following day, cleaned the remaining rooms, and got my friend's kitchen ready for Pesach. She is eternally grateful to those teenagers — and their generous parents — for all their help that year. (Avital likes to call that group of teenagers "The White Tornado" whenever she tells others what they did for her.)

▸ Invite those who are going through a difficult situation to your Seder. Do not make them feel that it will be a hardship in any way for you to have them over. Or, better yet, ask if they would prefer for you to come and make the Seder in their home, if they are taking care of an ill member of the family there.

On a Personal Note: Since my husband passed away, every year my brother and sister-in-law have very kindly invited us to come to them for the whole week of Pesach. And every year there is somebody who invariably says, "Oh, you're so lucky that you don't have to make Pesach and you get to go away instead!" Yes, I am extremely grateful that I do have family to go to for Pesach. But, lucky? Lucky is making Pesach and spending it at home together with your children... and your husband.

Example: A woman who has been childless for many years said the following: "I won't even go to a *shiur* during this time of year. Inevitably one of the women will ask a question about Pesach cleaning with children around and the whole rest of the *shiur* will somehow revolve around that one subject. Also, every year I always meet someone who tries to cheer me up by saying something to the effect of: 'You're so lucky that you don't have kids! You don't have to worry about re-doing things where you've already cleaned!' Some people don't realize how fortunate they are to have children. Believe me, it is infinitely harder to prepare for Pesach when you haven't been blessed with children than when you have!"

On a Personal Note: Our close friends, Yael and Binyamin Fisher, were planning to go away for the entire week of Pesach, to be with Yael's sister. Two days before Pesach, Yael called me and told me that she wanted to come over to talk to me. She said that she and Binyamin had learned that Dovid's condition had reached a critical stage, so they decided not to go away, but to stay and help us instead. They wanted to bring their family to our house and conduct our Seder.

My first reaction? I burst out laughing! "Yael, Pesach is two days away! How in the world are you going to make Pesach in your house AND cook for the Seder in forty-eight hours?"

She answered that she and Binyamin had discussed everything with our Rav, and he had explicitly instructed them concerning everything they could do to make kashering their kitchen and cleaning their house uncomplicated and manageable in a short time. I was simply stunned! But I really did need them that Pesach.

Binyamin called the next day to tell us that once people found out that they were staying for Pesach to be with the Feldbaums, food packages from friends began pouring in! People brought them kosher-for-Passover kugels, desserts, juice, dried fruit, and any canned goods they could spare so that this special couple could just concentrate on getting their house ready. Friends also brought them meals to eat before Pesach and sent their teenagers over to help clean and babysit. (To this day Binyamin loves to say that he doesn't know why people make such a fuss about getting ready for Pesach since they managed to do it in two days!)

Dovid was so ill that Pesach that he couldn't stay at either of the two Seders for very long. Binyamin, Yael, and their children walked over a mile each night in stormy weather to be with us. During the Seders I spent a lot of time running up and down the stairs to attend to Dovid, so Binyamin and Yael were the ones who made the Seders for our kids.

What an example of giving, kindness, and true friendship! This amazing family was willing and happy to cancel their plans to go away for Pesach at the last minute in exchange for a lot of hard work and self-sacrifice.

On Another Personal Note: I know a woman who, a few years ago, really and truly did not want to cook for the Pesach Seder. She had a newborn baby and two other little ones to take care of at home. Her husband was busy with a new job, and they had just moved into their first home. Everything seemed very difficult for her at the time and she didn't see how she could possibly handle making a Seder on top of it all. And so, the night before the Seder, after the search for *chametz*, she took a walk with her husband and told him in no uncertain terms that she was too exhausted and too busy to cook for a Seder the next night. He reassured her in his quiet way that whatever she did would be sufficient. If she was just up to putting matzah and wine on the table, he would prepare the rest of the meal. He was taking off the next day anyway, to help her. So she calmed down and together they made a simple, nice Pesach Seder for their family and her parents.

In retrospect, she looks back and cannot understand what on earth she was complaining about! The newborn baby was their first son after two daughters, and just a few weeks earlier they had celebrated his *bris*. What a tremendous *simchah*! How wonderful it was to be blessed with three healthy children! Her husband was being given more and more responsibilities at work and, even though he was traveling more, they were enjoying more financial security. Moreover, after moving from one country to another, they had finally been able to make a down payment on a new house on the same block as some wonderful religious families and near a few synagogues. Life was exciting and promising. Yet, at a time in her life when everything was going well, she was allowing the stress of bringing in Pesach to cast a cloud over every-thing.

I am the woman in this story. I had everything on a silver plat-ter and there I was "kvetching" and complaining. Now, whenever I hear women complaining before Pesach, I want to tell them: Don't worry about the work. Look around you and count your blessings instead!

SHAVUOS

Once Shavuos is over, all single parents can look back and see that they made it through yet another year of Jewish holidays. The following are things you can do to make a fam-ily's Shavuos easier:

▶ It is a custom on the night of Shavuos, for men and boys to stay up all night and study Torah. Often there are organized father-and-son learning sessions. If you know of a boy who does not have a father at home or in the same city, it is a tremendous *kindness* to invite him to join you or you and your son for these learning sessions. Try to take him un-der your wing and befriend him. (And don't assume that every other father of the boys classmates has already made this all-important offer!)

On a Personal Note: As my sons got a little older, they were encouraged by their teachers to go to the synagogue and take part in the learning for a few hours on Shavuos night. Many of the synagogues in our area arranged for speakers and spe-cial programs for youth. And, of course, there were plenty of treats given out!

It was absolutely heartwarming that so many of my sons' friends' fathers called and offered to take my boys to learn with them. I encouraged them to go and they really enjoyed being part of the Shavuos atmosphere with the others.

▶ Single fathers can certainly use a babysitter or some alternate sleeping arrangement for their young children on Shavuos night so that they can attend the study sessions too.

FAST DAYS

Fast days are usually a time when people living alone are forgotten. You can be considerate of others around these times in the following ways:

▶ Many people only think of extending meal invitations for Shabbos and Yom Tov, but not for the meal before or after a fast. Make it your business to remember others, particularly those who live alone, at these times of the year, too.

Example: A divorced woman said that she was so pleased to get an invitation from a family to break the fast with them after Yom Kippur that she was able to concentrate on her prayers much better that day.

Example: A single woman, who is very close with a particular family, is always looking for ways to express her gratitude to them for treating her like one of their own. Before every fast she eats at their home, and afterwards she hosts them at her home.

On a Personal Note: For my first fast without Dovid, I declined my neighbors' kind invitation to break the fast with them. But, saying Havdalah by myself and eating alone was a bit much for me. For the next fast, I accepted their invitation and it did make a big difference throughout the day, knowing that afterwards I would not be breaking the fast alone. I was looking forward to eating their delicious homemade rolls.

Chapter Seven:

Children Have Very Different Needs and Require Different Treatment

*O*ur children are a precious gift that Hashem gives into our hands for safe-keeping. Our primary responsibility towards them is to raise them in a healthy, safe, and nurturing environment. We try so hard to insulate them from all the hardships in life and from our personal problems so that they will grow up feeling totally secure and loved. We want them to enjoy their childhoods and try to keep them away from any unpleasantness. We even go as far as to hope that the greatest worry they will ever experience while growing up will be over some exam for which they must study.

I so much wanted that for my children. Yet, as it turned out, they suffered a blow so severe that it changed their lives forever. As hard as the death of a spouse is, it cannot compare to the trauma of losing a parent at such a young age. My children are not "sheltered" anymore.

Sometimes people will make a completely inappropriate remark in front of them or do something that hurts their feelings. The purpose of this chapter is to educate the reader about what things are helpful and what are harmful to children who are going through such stressful times.

179

FOR THE CHILDREN'S SAKE

In the months after my husband died, I was in such pain that I just wanted to pull my blanket over my head and hide from the world. Yet because I had children, I had to pull myself out of bed every morning. I knew that my responsibilities towards them had not ended with the loss of my husband. On the contrary, I was the only parent they had now. That knowledge gave me the strength to do what had to be done, to take care of them while putting aside my personal pain.

Example: Pesha, a young widow, was asked to visit Zissi and offer her some words of comfort after she lost her husband. As it turned out, the grieving widow was seriously falling apart. When Pesha came home, she said, "The situation there is just terrible. When I lost my husband, my children just lost their father. Over there, the children have lost both their father and their mother."

PROTECTING THE CHILDREN

When couples go through a crisis and need to make major decisions in order to deal with it, children are often left out of the proceedings. Ultimately the parents inform the children what is going on and what they have decided, but until then the children feel the tension, but do not understand. It affects the whole family's well-being and the children suffer greatly from it. They feel as though their security is being threatened.

It is very difficult to think everything through while under stress. Because we want to do what is right for our children, we need to recognize the thin line between protecting them and letting them know what is going on so that they won't feel frightened. Our instincts tells us that they know something is not right, but we aren't sure how much they have noticed and understood. As it turns out, many times it is a lot more than we realize.

Children should be told from the beginning — on a level that they are able to understand — what is causing the tension in their home. They do not have to know every detail; just keep the lines of communication open so that they will feel free to ask questions. It is always best to have an honest dialogue with them, but they have to be spoken to at their level, in a calm and caring manner.

When a parent is going through a serious illness, the children basically need to know and be assured of the following things:

- ▶ What is going on (told to them on their level, of course)
- ▶ That even though things are a little different at home, they are still very much loved
- ▶ That things may be a little different now, but Mommy and Daddy will do their very best to make their home environment as normal as possible
- ▶ That the illness has nothing to do with anything they did and is certainly not their fault
- ▶ That no matter what happens in the future, they will always be well-cared for and loved

One woman who lost her father at an early age said that when he was ill her house was always draped in secrecy and she was not told anything about his illness. She described the effect this had on her throughout her life: She developed an extremely suspicious nature and felt that she couldn't trust adults.

A man who lost his mother at an early age said that he was glad his parents told him about his mother's illness soon after it was diagnosed. He said that it was obvious to him that his mother was not well, and his parents' openness about the situation made it much easier for him to deal with.

Do not wait to talk to your child until he begins to ask questions. When a parent is not able to work a full day, or prepare meals, or join Sunday outings, or stops going to the *minyan* in the morning that he always attended, and there are numerous phone calls and whispered conversations, any normal child is bound to notice. A discussion with him, however, does not have to take place the week of the diagnosis, if you and your spouse need a little time to decide how best to handle the situation.

It is important to get guidance on how to handle this critical issue with your children. Make an appointment with a competent child psychologist and ask him what the appropriate approach with each one of your children should be.

Obviously, with teenagers the explanations need to be much more specific. Since they are at such a precarious age, a therapist or knowledgeable counselor can be immensely helpful in advising you about how much to tell them and how to go about it. If they seem overwhelmed with worry, they may benefit from professional help for a while.

As one woman said to her husband while waiting for his test results, "The unknown is the worst. Once we know what we are dealing with we can conquer our fears and move on from there." This same statement can apply to children's fears as well.

On a Personal Note: The week I came home from sitting *Shivah* in Israel, I took my daughters to see a licensed family and child therapist who specializes in grief therapy. I was very fortunate to find an extremely capable Orthodox Jewish woman with our Torah values and superb qualifications. They were able to discuss with her all they had seen and heard and were able to trust her with their innermost feelings about the loss of their father.

I learned that there was also the possibility of going to family sessions, in which everyone in the family takes part.

Children can also join a group with others who are their own age. One friend who sent her young children to this type of group said that each child made a special family photo album that included pictures, information about their deceased parent, and their personal comments on the subject. She noted that, years later, her children still look at their precious albums.

Example: Libby and her husband Dov were informed by his insurance company that some of his treatments and medical procedures could be provided at home. The couple decided to use this option whenever possible.

The first few times that Dov had an IV treatment in his bedroom, both parents were adamant that their young children not be allowed in the room. Finally, their daughter Temima asked her mother, "Just what is that nurse doing in there to my Tatti?"

Libby did not know how to handle the situation so she contacted her children's physician. The doctor advised Libby to open the bedroom door wide and let the children see what was going on. He said that they would be much more fearful not knowing what was going on inside.

The next time the nurse came, the door stayed wide open. With the arm that was not hooked up to the IV, Dov beckoned his children to come into the room. His son just smiled and ran away, but his daughter climbed onto the bed to lie down by her father. The nurse was informed ahead of time about their new policy and she was very patient about answering all of Temima's questions. Temima then went into the other room, took one of her books, and crawled right back into her father's welcoming arm. They lay side-by-side and read together.

In the ensuing months, when she was not in school or camp, Temima would read quietly alongside her father while he had the IV in his arm. She was not in the room whenever he had the IV inserted or taken out. And Dov made sure to keep a ready supply of candy hidden away to share with Temima whenever she came to visit him!

DON'T TALK ABOUT THE DETAILS OF THE ILLNESS IN FRONT OF THE CHILDREN

This is so important! Please make sure that "adult conversations" stay between adults. Children are like magicians — they can make themselves invisible when any adult conversation is going on. So be careful. They absorb all that they hear, and then attach their own meaning to it.

When children enter a room where an adult conversation is taking place, in most instances the adults keep right on talking without giving it a second thought. This is a very grave mistake because the subject matter can really upset the children. Like a water faucet, such a conversation should be turned off before too much comes out!

Children should definitely not be permitted to listen to conversations about medical costs, reactions to drugs, or how some family members are coping with the news, etc. They will only be frightened by information that they do not understand. Also, seeing an adult look upset and frightened about the situation can terrify a child. At this time, the children need love and support — not more things to worry about.

What about those friends and acquaintances who tearfully confront the wife or husband of a seriously ill person and his/her children in a public place? How are these mothers and fathers to react with their children (and everyone else) watching? (Even if their children are not with them, public areas are no place for private, emotional encounters.) Do not put others in that predicament! They are doing their best to hold up in public, so don't expect to have a heartfelt conversation with them in the middle of the grocery store, especially with their children in tow!

Also, do not worry that by not alluding to their situation in public, they will think you are callous and heartless. On the contrary, they will be grateful not be put in an uncomfortable situation in front of everyone. If you have something personal to say, send a card or a note, call on the telephone and ask if it is a good time to talk for a few minutes, or make a date to go to their home and tell them there. This is so much more appreciated than trying to discuss personal issues in front of the children or anyone else who happens to be nearby.

On a Personal Note: I was at a *Kiddush* with Dovid and the children. Thankfully, he was sitting down on the other side of the room while I was helping the children with their plates, when an acquaintance accosted me. "Oh, Becca," she said, "I just heard the terrible news about your husband being sick! It must be so awful for you, with young children and all! How terrible! What are you going to do?"

My six-year-old was standing right next to me, and this woman's words terrified her.

I calmly turned to the woman and replied, "Actually, we are all doing fine right now and really enjoying this wonderful *Kiddush!*" Then I turned away from her and quickly, albeit rudely on my part, ended the conversation.

My daughter, who had turned pale, asked me, "Why did she say that to you about Tatti?"

I replied, "She just found out that Tatti is not well, but we have known that for a long time. Remember, I told you we just have to take each week as it comes and, *baruch Hashem*, Tatti had a good week this week, right?" My daughter nodded in agreement and some of the color began to return to her face.

Of course, it ruined the *Kiddush* for me, as I had been in such a good mood before because Dovid's week HAD been good. But what it did to me was minor in comparison to what it had done to my little girl.

SHOULD YOU MENTION A DECEASED PARENT IN FRONT OF A CHILD?

There is a common misconception that when a child loses a parent, it is best not to mention that parent ever again. Nothing could be farther from the truth. Pretending the parent never existed does the child far more harm than good. Even very young children who lose a parent at an age when they cannot remember him very well still find comfort in seeing photographs and talking about him. Thoughts of this parent are always on the "back burner" of their mind. As one widow said, "My youngest daughter was three years old when her father died. Before her Bas Mitzvah, her class was asked to write a biography on anyone in their family. My daughter did not hesitate to say she wanted to write a paper about her father. No matter what anyone says, kids do not want to forget!"

Children also want to find a way to stay connected to that parent. They do this by: going into the same profession as that parent, taking up a hobby that parent liked, learning to play the same musical instrument that parent played, etc. Others like to cook that parent's favorite meal and serve it on special occasions, or wear the same perfume or cologne that the parent wore, or even volunteer for the same charity organization that the parent was active in.

Example: Gilda's father passed away when she was in elementary school. For her birthday the following year, one of her friends gave her a diary. On her own, Gilda decided to make it a "Dear Daddy" diary. Every night she wrote in it to tell him about her day — whether it was just a few lines or a few pages!

As a teenager, Gilda still writes in her diary and even takes it with her whenever she spends the night away. She spoke about how important this is to her. "I am now writing in my fourth diary to my father. It gives me a tremendous feeling of peace to let him in on all the good and bad times in my life. A lot of things I write to him are very personal — just between the two of us. I am not still mourning his loss. Instead I am sharing my life him. I lost him at such a young age that this diary really lets me stay connected to him. In this way, it keeps his memory alive for me.

"If someone keeps this kind of diary, no one else should ever ask to read it. I'm not sure, but maybe I'll share it with my own children someday."

When children lose a sibling or friend to whom they were extremely close, they do not want to forget that person either.

Example: The Bernstein's lost a young child after a serious illness only a few months before their oldest daughter Chana's wedding. They tried to be as happy as they could for Chana's sake, but they did not think they would be able to concentrate on her *simchah* exclusively, without thinking about their beloved daughter who had died.

A few days before her wedding, Chana told her parents that she wanted to walk down the aisle to a popular tune that had her sister's name prominently featured in the lyrics. She said that she knew that everyone would be thinking about her younger sister anyway, and she so much wanted to try and make her a part of the wedding.

And so, as the Bernsteins happily walked Chana down the aisle, they pretended not to notice the gasps and the flow of tears from the people who recognized the tune and knew what the words were. Because their special daughter was willing to share her *simchah* with her sister and publicly demonstrate how much she was missed, it made things more comfortable for the people who were attending the wedding too.

LET YOUR CHILD CONTINUE
TO HAVE A CHILDHOOD

After the death of a parent, children still need to have a normal childhood. They must feel safe, protected, and loved at home. It is important to understand that teenagers are still children and need to be regarded as such. They should never be burdened with assuming the responsibilities of the deceased parent. This can stunt their emotional growth by forcing them to skip an important developmental step that will lead to their becoming whole, emotionally healthy adults.

A young boy who has lost his father should never be told that he is now "the man of the house." If he starts thinking about all the new responsibilities he is expected to assume as the "father," he will feel overwhelmed and frightened. A teenage boy should never be given the impression that he is now on equal footing with the remaining parent. That will lead him to start acting as if he is in charge, when he is not prepared for such a responsibility. That also might lead him to act disrespectfully toward his parent if they disagree about something.

The same rule applies to girls who have lost a parent, especially a mother. Teenage daughters should not be encouraged to become the replacement mother. Younger siblings will not want their sister suddenly telling them what to do; they will not accept her authority. It will also pile responsibilities on her that she is not prepared for and deprive her of the rest of her childhood. The remaining parent has to assume both parental roles in the household and be careful not to make any of the children into a partner.

This is not to say that it is harmful for the children to do more chores around the house. That is part of pulling together as a family, with everyone helping out. But it is important that children not be given too many chores. They need to have a healthy childhood in which they still have time to get together with their friends, do their homework properly, and participate in extracurricular activities.

Also, unless there are unusual, extenuating circumstances, children should not be separated from their remaining parent. By not seeing their parent, they could develop the devastating fear that something terrible is happening to him/her too.

If the parent is too distraught to handle the needs of the children at the moment, an adult who has a close relationship with them should become heavily involved in the home situation until things improve. The children will be needing plenty of empathy and attention at this time.

Widows and widowers must also be very careful not to make their children feel guilty in any way, giving them the impression that they now have a duty to take care of, and protect, the remaining parent. If you see this happening in a family, please have a close relative or friend intervene on the children's behalf.

WHEN YOUR CHILD'S FRIEND LOSES A PARENT

If your child's friend loses a parent, he might need your advice on how to treat that friend. If you have never dealt with this situation before, you may not be sure of what's best to tell him. The following people might be able to advise you or refer you to someone more experienced with this:

- ▶ A Rabbi or Rebbetzin
- ▶ A teacher or guidance counselor at the school your child attends
- ▶ A social worker who is involved with such issues
- ▶ A close friend or family member who has suffered a major loss in the past
- ▶ Someone active in the Bikkur Cholim organization in your city

▶ A compassionate doctor
▶ A grief therapist or counselor

Not every Rabbi, social worker, or teacher will be able to advise you. Just because a person has a title in front of or after his name, it does not mean that he knows how you should deal with every situation. Pick someone who has dealt successfully with these issues before. It should be someone you respect because of his sensitivity and compassion towards others.

The way you handle this situation the first time can have far-reaching effects on your child. That is why it is of paramount importance that your child have the opportunity to express his concerns to an adult who can answer his questions properly. (A child may prefer to talk to someone other than his parent; don't make him feel disloyal if he chooses someone else.)

Whatever you do, do not "sweep your child's questions under the rug," especially if this is his first encounter with such a tragedy. Your child might be afraid to play with the friend who lost a parent for fear that his friend might die too. He might start worrying for his own safety, or for yours. These are normal fears that children have.

Create an atmosphere in which your child can feel free to come and express his concerns to you. Death is a frightening subject for an adult, so you can well imagine what must go through a child's mind when he has no one to answer his questions or at least to acknowledge them.

Let your child know if you have gone for guidance on this. He will benefit from learning that asking for advice on how to deal with something is nothing to be ashamed of.

On a Personal Note: When I sat *Shivah* in Israel, my sons (aged four and two) stayed in the United States for three weeks with our close friends, Adina and Meir Lerman. I told the boys about their father's death before I left for Israel, but being so young, I don't know how fully they understood what I was saying.

Adina and Meir really went out of their way to ask various people how to handle the questions that the boys might ask. They wanted to be completely prepared.

One night at the dinner table, my oldest son Moshe asked them, "Mommy said that Tatti died. Is it true? Is my Tatti really dead?"

Adina and Meir told me that they took a deep breath and explained to him the following: Yes, Tatti was dead, but he was no longer sick. He was healthy in Heaven with Hashem.

They continued, telling Moshe that he would always be loved by the friends and family that were here, that everyone cared about him and his family very much, and he could always come to them whenever he had a problem. They said that he looked at them with a very serious expression on his face the whole time.

After they finished with all of their explanations and reassurances, Moshe said to them, "Can I ask you one more question?"

"Moshe, you can ask anything you want to know at any time. We are always here for you," Adina responded.

"Aunt Adina," Moshe continued, "do I have to eat the crust on my bread?"

That was the first and last time Moshe brought up the topic about his father's death when I was in Israel! The Lermans felt confident that Moshe understood two important points: where his father was, and that many people cared about him and his family. (And also that he didn't have to finish the crust on his bread!)

Example: Elaine is a widow. Once, her son, Zev, invited a friend over who had never been to his house before. They picked him up and the two boys went skipping up the walk together, having a very animated conversation. When they came to the front door, the friend ran back to Elaine and excitedly asked, "Is it true that Zev's Daddy died? He's dead, right? He's not in the house?"

Elaine looked at this small child and saw the honesty and inquisitiveness in his face. Her son was standing nearby with an embarrassed grin on his face. He clearly did not know how to react.

Elaine told this friend that Zev's Daddy had died and was in Heaven, but the love that he had for Zev was in their house and would always be with Zev wherever he lived.

"That's neat!" exclaimed the friend, and the two boys then bounded into the house.

Elaine told me that was the first (and last) time she had seen someone so excited that her husband had died!

On a Personal Note: Along these same lines is another "neat" story that happened to my younger son Michoel Simcha. Michoel came home from school one day and said that he had something very exciting to tell me. His English teacher had given them the spelling words for that week and then asked the boys to raise their hands if they knew the meaning of the different words.

"One of the words was widow, Mommy, and I was the only boy in the class who raised my hand!" he told me enthusiastically. "I told the whole class that a widow is a lady whose husband is dead, and my mommy is a widow!

"The teacher said that I was right and I told her that my mommy is the only widow in the whole class! Isn't that neat?"

What else could I do but agree with him that it was nice that we were the stars of his classroom that day?

It is the parents' responsibility to teach their children to treat a child or teenager who has lost his parent with consideration. I cite two true stories below: The first shows a child who was not taught to have the proper respect for another's feelings, and the second shows a teenager teaching her friend to appreciate the father that she has.

Example: Frima's father died when she was very young. When she was in high school, her school sponsored a Shabbaton for the tenth-graders, and those students who did not live nearby were placed in their classmates' homes for Shabbos. They were to eat and sleep at their host's home on Friday night, and then spend Shabbos day together at the school, for prayer services, meals, and various activities.

Frima, who lived near the school, invited one of her classmates, who lived on the other side of town, to stay with her. The girl bluntly replied, "I don't go to homes where there isn't a father to make *Kiddush*."

Frima said that her friend's insensitivity left her weeping for weeks.

On a Personal Note: Chavi Horowitz, a very special young woman who was a "helper" in our home for many years, told me the following story:

One day she was waiting with a classmate by the public telephone at her seminary in Israel, since both of them were expecting calls from their families in America. The classmate turned to Chavi and said, "I hope my mother will be on the line, because I just don't like talking to my father. I have nothing to say to him." Chavi (who lost her father at the age of four) replied to this girl, "I would give anything in the world to be able to have a conversation with MY father."

GOING BACK TO SCHOOL AFTER A DEATH

After the death of a close family member, young children as well as teenagers go through an emotionally painful readjustment process upon returning to school. Children must face their teachers and friends day after day, even though they are feeling disoriented and sad.

It takes time for a child to learn how to handle all of his different feelings. He must go to school (where nothing has changed for anyone else) and then he must return to a home that has undergone a major upheaval, where someone he loved very much is now gone.

The best way school administrators can help these children is to try to be as prepared as possible to handle the situation. Principals, teachers, and other staff members should be open to getting advice from professionals in the field of grief therapy for children.

Example: One widow told me that her children's teachers called her up after a grief counselor had spoken with them a few weeks after her husband passed away. They told her how much they had learned and assured her that they now felt much better equipped to deal with the situation.

Teachers should also be willing to discuss with their students how to be considerate of a fellow student who has lost a member of his family. A grief counselor can speak to the students if the teacher is more comfortable with that arrangement.

If the loss occurred during a summer camp session, the camp's administration and the child's counselor should take it upon themselves to find out what to do for the child. The same holds true for youth group leaders. One point that should be stressed is how difficult Shabbos is for the child during the first year.

All of the teenagers I spoke with emphasized the importance of having these professionals speak with their teachers and classmates before the child returns to school. They agreed that this made a big difference in how quickly they adapted to being back.

If a child seems overly concerned about returning to school, it is advisable that he speak to a professional. The goal is to make his re-entry into school life as pain-free as possible.

Note: Car-pool drivers need to remember that children over the age of Bar Mitzvah who are in mourning are not permitted to listen to music for the year. So make sure you turn off your music tapes. You can put on talking tapes instead, if you wish. A few teenagers have told me that because their car-pool driver wasn't sensitive to this, they had to ask him politely to turn the music off and so their day got off to a bad start just by having to deal with this issue first thing in the morning.

Many of the following suggestions were made by my daughters' grief counselor. They are intended to serve as guidelines, but they cannot take the place of discussing individual cases with a trained professional.

(In order not to clutter what is written below with too many pronouns, let us assume that the child we are talking about is female.)

The First Day Back

On the child's first day back, she should walk into school with a good friend. She will definitely feel more comfortable that way.

Advice for classmates and teachers: Do not greet her effusively when you see her in the hallway for the first time. She does not want to be fussed over or treated differently in front of everyone. Welcome her back quietly and privately. It is all right to tell her how happy you are to have her back in school or that you missed her, but be careful not to stare at her (or you can avoid looking at her altogether). Be careful not to whisper behind her back either, as it is very likely that she will overhear what you say. Any overt affection on your part might cause her to cry, so assess the situation before you hug her or put your arm around her shoulder.

Example: Dina sat *Shivah* for her father and returned to her high school the following week. Her friends and teachers were being extremely nice and supportive, but still her stomach was tied up in knots!

When Dina opened her locker, she saw a big card taped on the inside of the door. On the front of it was a teddy bear with his arms extended. Printed inside were the words: "Here is a hug that is just for you!" Then there was a personal message from Tziona, an acquaintance who had lost her father a few years before: "Whenever you need a hug, come to me because I know just how you feel!"

Dina said that everything else about the first day she went back to school is a big blank in her mind, except for this thoughtful gesture from a girl she hardly knew.

Catching Up on Schoolwork

If there is schoolwork that has to be made up, teachers should not discuss it on the first day back. It's a hard day for her to concentrate in general. Tell her a few days or a week later, once she appears to have settled in.

Mentioning the Loss

The teacher and the class should take their cues from the child about mentioning her loss. The most important thing at this time is to try and behave as normally as possible and to treat her the same as before. She has enough changes going on at home to deal with, so stability at school is a welcome thing.

Show Acceptance

The first couple of weeks after a death in the family, children need a lot of acceptance. Some children may experience different forms of regression in terms of their schoolwork or social behavior. (This is especially true of middle-school students.) Try not to show too many signs of disapproval, since they may not be doing it consciously. Encourage them to do a lot of quiet reading. This is very soothing and can help calm down their inner emotional turmoil. Also, do not pressure them at this time with too much responsibility.

After a death in the family, children need to feel emotionally safe. The teacher and the students should let the child know, as unobtrusively as possible, that they do not think any differently about her since she lost a parent. Unfortunately, she might feel that she is tainted now. But the more accepted the child is made to feel, the less inferior she will feel.

Permit the Student "Time Out"

It is beneficial when the Rebbe or main teacher talks to the child before she comes back to school. She should be told that any time she is feeling overwhelmed, she has permission to leave the classroom for a few minutes. A simple hand sign on the student's part will let the teacher know she is taking a "time out."

They should agree on a prearranged appropriate place where she can go for a few minutes of quiet time — the main office, the infirmary, a lounge area, etc. School staff should also be told about this arrangement so that they don't say anything to embarrass the child. The approximate amount of time the student is permitted to remain out of class should be specified, and of course, this depends on her age. (A classmate should be assigned to take notes for this student while she is out, and to fill her in later on what she missed.)

The class can be told about this prearrangement if the teacher thinks it is beneficial for them to know, but the teacher should use common sense in deciding this. Again, the most important thing to the child is that she goes back to being "one of the gang" again, and not some outsider just because her parent died.

On a Personal Note: A few weeks after we came back from Israel, my daughters started calling me from school, begging me to come and pick them up. They were learning *Sefer Bereishis* (the Book of Genesis), and every time a Forefather died and was buried in Israel it brought back many vivid memories for them.

Fortunately, they had a very compassionate and understanding elementary school principal, who sat down with them and told them that during school hours they really should stay in school. He explained to them that if they felt upset or needed to cry, they could privately signal their teacher and she would let them leave the classroom and come straight to his office!

My youngest daughter did this only once or twice, but my older daughter did it quite a few times. She would sit there for half an hour or less — quietly reading or coloring — and then return to class. (Wisely, the principal did not try to pressure her into talking.) Just knowing that she could take some quiet "time out" when she was feeling upset about her father gave her a tremendous feeling of relief.

Watch What You Say

When a child has recently suffered a terrible loss, it is important not to throw "religious platitudes" at her. The child's confusion and anger about her loss need to be addressed by the appropriate person, and at this point it might be harmful for anyone else to try to impose on her a pat religious interpretation of the tragedy. No matter how well-meaning a person might be, the child, in the depth of her grief, may not be ready to hear such explanations. On the other hand, definitely talk about such things with her if she brings up the subject.

Be careful not to give the child the impression that her deceased parent is watching her all the time from Heaven! This will make her feel that she is constantly being examined "under a microscope" from up above — an image that will frighten her. (In some cases, feeling under surveillance like this can cause great anxiety and lead to physical problems like ticks, gastrointestinal upsets, bedwetting, etc.) If she misbehaves, do not tell her that her parent in Heaven is angry with her. Every once in a while it is acceptable to convey to the child that her parent is proud of her when she does something good, or gets a good grade, or wins a sports tournament, etc. But limit when you do this so that she will not imagine that her parent is perpetually judging her. It is better to just reassure the child in general terms that her parent's unconditional love will always be there for her.

When Sensitive Subject Matter Is Discussed in Class

When a teacher presents material in class, especially about Shabbos or Yom Tov, she should be especially careful about how she does it. For instance, she can say that the "father or other head of the household" recites *Kiddush* instead of saying that only the father does, and no one will feel left out.

When discussing *halachos* that apply exclusively to either a father or a mother, try asking the child ahead of time outside of class if she has any ideas about how you should present the subject matter.

If you are discussing anything whatsoever that has to do with dying, death, or resurrection of the dead, do not ask the child to read aloud the source material on the subject. Certainly do not ask her opinion on what was just read, unless she volunteers to comment on it. Also, in the middle of such a discussion, you should refrain from looking at the student to check how she is reacting; that just draws more attention to the student and causes others to look at her too.

A Picture of the Parent Who Died

Many children like to have a picture of the parent who died taped to their locker door, desk, or main notebook. This visual reminder comforts and calms them. (A competent grief counselor can suggest other tips that will help keep the child feeling reassured throughout the day.)

The Parent's Yahrtzeit

At the beginning of the school year, an efficient school office should inform all of the teachers when a parent's *yahrtzeit* (anniversary of the day of death) is for any student in their class. One of the reasons for this is so that school trips and major activities will not be scheduled for then. Another reason is that the parent's *yahrtzeit* is a very upsetting time for a child.

She might start acting differently a week or so beforehand: not paying attention, picking fights with classmates, talking back to authority figures, or even having an emotional outburst about nothing in particular. Probably, she is venting anger because she misses her parent, or she is jealous of her other classmates who have both parents, or maybe she is dreading what things will be like at home on the day of the *yahrtzeit*.

If the teacher is informed of when the *yahrtzeit* is, she can better understand and deal with the child's change in behavior. Some suggestions regarding this are:

▶ Take the child aside and speak with her privately in a friendly manner. Let her know that you are aware of her profound loss and that you realize that she is probably in a lot of emotional pain. If you have experienced a similar loss, you can share this with the child, if you wish. This is a much better tactic to use than just telling her to behave.

▶ Tell the child nicely, but firmly, that she has a right to be sad, but that doesn't mean that she has a right to disrupt the class because she feels bad. You can arrange a private signal between the two of you that you will use to surreptitiously indicate that her behavior is getting out of hand. Speak to her in a manner that shows you mean business, but your voice should not show any trace of anger...only compassion.

▶ Show empathy and understanding. The child will most likely try to behave once she knows that you are really trying to understand and help her through this difficult time. (By the way, do not bring up any of this as a precautionary measure if the child is not exhibiting any signs of misbehavior.)

▶ If these suggestions do not seem to be working, a parent or principal may have to get involved. But make sure that whoever speaks to her does not show any anger or reject the child in any way.

▶ Do not expect this child to completely open up and tell you all her thoughts or feelings. Remember, it is not the teacher's place to be a student's best friend. You are there to help and to guide. If you can accomplish that, you have done a lot. (If the student does pour out her heart to you, there is a good chance that she will feel uncomfortable towards you for some time afterwards.)

Example: Yaffa Jacobi had been excitedly looking forward to her class "mystery trip" for weeks. Her school never told the girls in advance where they would be going, only on which day it would take place.

Finally the permission slips were passed out and Yaffa brought hers home for her mother to sign. As her mother, Cheryl, looked over the information, her heart skipped a beat. She then had the unpleasant task of informing Yaffa that the date of the trip coincided with her father's *yahrtzeit*. Of all the days in the school year to pick!

Cheryl called her Rabbi about the situation and asked him what to do. He was extremely sympathetic, but told her that participating in such an activity was just not the proper thing to do on a parent's *yahrtzeit*. (Some individuals even fast on that day.)

As soon as Yaffa left for school the following day, Cheryl called the vice-principal of her school and told him about the date they had chosen. "Oh, no!" he exclaimed.

"I know that I'm asking a lot," she continued, "but is there any way you can postpone the trip a week or even a day so that Yaffa can go too?" The vice-principal told her that he would get back to her about it.

That afternoon, Cheryl received a call at work. The vice-principal said, "Mrs. Jacobi, I have good news! When I re-layed your message to the principal, he immediately told his secretary to call the bus company and find out whether they would have buses and drivers available on the following day. After they said it wasn't a problem, I told your daughter privately about your call and explained that we were not going to tell any of her classmates or teachers what was going on, but we were simply going to ask if changing the date would present a problem for any of them. All of them said that it was fine. So your daughter will be able go on the class trip!"

Cheryl told him how much she appreciated what they had done. Later that day, Yaffa came bursting into the house and ran to hug her mother. "Mommy," she said, "thank you so, so, so much!"

As a postscript to this story, when Cheryl called her Rabbi and told him what the principals had done, he exclaimed, "*Baruch Hashem*! It was bothering me the whole day that I had to tell your daughter that she couldn't go. I was going to ask you if you would mind my calling the principal about changing the date, but you beat me to it, Mrs. Jacobi. I want you to know that those principals really did the right thing. I'm going to call them right now and tell them so!"

*   *   *

RAIZEL'S STORY:
REFLECTIONS ON LOSING MY FATHER

I asked my oldest daughter Raizel to write down a few of her thoughts and memories about losing her father, with an eye toward explaining what people did that was helpful and what was painful. She was seven years old when Dovid died and she wrote this when she was fourteen.

The Last Year

Toward the end of Tatti's life, he got sicker and I became scared. I remember having a lot of questions. I could not fit them all into words. Many of my questions were Why? Why couldn't Tatti come play with us? Why did he need to lie on the couch? Why did we have to pull over onto the side of the road when he wasn't feeling well and he couldn't concentrate on driving? Why, why, why?

I think it might have been less frightening if somebody had explained to me what was going on. I didn't need a lengthy answer, just a brief explanation of what was happening to Tatti. You might think a child could not grasp a concept like death, and in a way you are right. But at least we would know there were answers. I might not have understood, but at least things wouldn't have been so foggy. At times what a child imagines is worse than the truth.

Teachers

Baruch Hashem, I've had wonderful teachers; and there were some who really went out of their way to make sure I was all right. The things they did made a big impression on me and helped me a lot during hard times.

Example: The year Tatti died, I was in second grade. In my Chumash class we were up to the chapter where Yaakov dies. However, the Torah does not just mention it, but rather goes into all the details of what the Tribes went through to give Yaakov a proper burial.

Before we started the chapter my teacher, Mrs. Herman, called me out of class. She told me what we were going to learn. Then she said, "If anything I teach during class upsets you, feel free to leave."

Example: After Tatti died, my teacher from the year before, Mrs. Brown, told me during recess, "If you ever need someone to talk to, Raizel, I am here for you." I don't believe I even thanked her for being so thoughtful, especially since she was no longer my teacher. But those few seconds meant the world to me!

I never did take advantage of those opportunities, but it was a wonderful feeling to know my teachers had thought of me and were so sensitive to my feelings. The fact that they cared made a big difference. And, I always knew if worse came to worst, they would be there for me. That is the most wonderful feeling you can give a child going through a hard time.

A Teacher's Mistake

I could not seem to grasp a math concept in class. Confused, I asked the teacher to try to explain it in a different way. She agreed, and asked me what my father does for a living. I was not sure what to answer, so I was quiet. Quickly the teacher realized her mistake and said, "Let's say someone is a doctor..."

That is the best way for a teacher to correct a blunder. The teacher should not apologize in front of the class because it makes the child feel awkward. Also, anyone in class who does not know the child's personal situation will ask about it. I think you get the idea. If the teacher would like to apologize afterwards, that is okay, but it's not at all necessary. We know it was a mistake.

During another class we were discussing how one must be nice to a widow. My teacher asked me to read where it says to do that in the *Chumash*. I felt very awkward and I could see out of the corner of my eye that everyone was giving me pitiful glances. I knew what they were thinking: "Oh poor Raizel, her mother is in that situation." I remember squirming in my seat, glancing at the clock, and praying for class to end so I could escape my "pitiful situation." I know this teacher didn't purposely call on me, and I don't blame her.

When discussing topics related to death or dying, don't look at us or call on us. It makes us feel uncomfortable. Sometimes discussions about death or sickness brought back bad memories or upset me. I greatly appreciated when the teacher left me alone. I just wanted to stare at my notebook, collect my thoughts, and move on.

Mah Nishtanah

While doing my homework, I happened to ask my brother what he was learning in school. Since it was almost Pesach, I asked if he was learning the *"Mah Nishtanah"* (The Four Questions asked at the Seder). He sighed and nodded.

I was puzzled by his sad response, so I asked him if anything was the matter. My brother said, "We're learning the *Mah Nishtanah* in Yiddish. To start it off, we are supposed to say "Tatti"...but my Tatti is dead, so how will I say it to him?"

I told my mother, who immediately called his Rebbe. The Rebbe was very nice and understanding, and the first thing the next morning he told my brother that he didn't have to start off the *Mah Nishtanah* with "Tatti."

Now, who would have thought that was what had been bothering my brother? Not many of us. But maybe if you try to be more alert about each lesson, you'll find little things that might best be taught in a different way.

I also want to add here that the subject of saying "Tatti" at the start of the *Mah Nishtanah* was brought up in my brother's car pool. One of the younger boys said that his father told him that "Tatti" did not refer to someone's father, but to Hashem, our Father in Heaven. My brother was so happy to hear this explanation. It just shows how one child can make another child feel so much better about things!

Pity vs. Compassion

It may sound strange, but we would like to be shown some compassion. I wouldn't call it pity, for there is a big line between pity and compassion. Pity is what you feel for someone whose tragic situation you can't change. For instance, you can't bring my Tatti back. Compassion is a mixture of understanding and sensitivity.

When do we want compassion? During hard times, even when the hard time has nothing to do with the loss of our parent. You must understand that, for me, something is always missing. My Tatti is not here and it affects my everyday life. Yet, as the years go on, it has become easier to accept.

There is one thing I could never stand — and that is to be pitied. When adults would ask me something about my father I would have to explain to them that he died. I could see their eyes soften and then they would say to me, "I'm so sorry." That's the right reaction to have. But sometimes I would see them go off whispering, and then they would give me sympathetic glances. That always upset me. I always wanted to tell them: "I don't need your pity. I have a wonderful life! Let me enjoy it without having to be constantly reminded about the unfortunate parts!"

And worst of all was when I would say something sort of hinting that my father died or just come out and mention it, and others would pretend that I didn't say a thing. Believe me, it was just as uncomfortable for me to say this as it was for you to hear it. At least acknowledge the fact that you heard what I said. Then, of course, a simple condolence would be fine. Please don't put me through a lot of lengthy questions about what happened.

An Adult's Mistake

This happened a little more than a year after Tatti died. We were at Mommy's friend's house, and I can't remember what the grown-ups were talking about when Mommy's friend suddenly said to her, "Wouldn't it be wonderful if you got remarried?" Suddenly it hit me — Mommy can get remarried! I had never considered that before. It was very frightening. Would we just replace Tatti? And what would happen when Mashiach came and the dead came to life?

This incident might seem small, but I was upset about it for a week or so. Certain subjects should never be brought up in front of kids.

Friends of All Ages

I have the most wonderful friends! They did not analyze me or try to understand what I was going through, but, instead, they just listened when I wanted to talk.

I have always believed my friends understood me better than any grown-up. And so, when I was brought to a grief therapist, I was surprised that everyone expected me to tell things to a complete stranger. But going really helped me deal with my feelings. Sometimes I would have rather not gone to her because I wanted to pretend that it had not happened and everything was all right. She helped me recognize why I was upset about certain things, when I would have preferred not to think about it.

Some friends and I were having a sleepover party. We had invited a girl who was relatively new to town, Ilana. During our party, Ilana asked me what my father does. Tatti had died a year-and-a-half before. I hardly ever discussed it, so when she brought it up everyone became quiet. Maybe it was because I was in such a good mood or maybe because I knew she didn't mean to hurt me that I was able to say the words, "My Tatti died." That was the first time I actually told a friend that my father died.

Father's Day

In school we always make a present for our fathers for Father's Day. The year Tatti died, I overheard two of my classmates talking.

"Well, you heard."

"Heard what?"

"We can't make a Father's Day present this year because someone's father died, and she'll probably cry 'cause she won't have anyone to give it to."

I knew exactly who they were talking about — ME! I never thought I had no one to give my present to. I simply thought I could give it to my Grandpa. What hurt the most was that I realized how insensitive people could be.

Note: We did end up making a Father's Day present and I proudly shipped mine all the way to Little Rock, Arkansas for my Grandpa to enjoy.

A Friend's Mistake

My friend Shoshy was telling a group of girls at school how she and her father have a close relationship. Some of the girls standing around said they weren't close to their fathers at all and they thought it was weird that she was.

Upset, Shoshy left the room and my friend and I followed her. Once we got to the hallway, she turned to us and asked, "Don't you talk to your father?"

My friend nodded. Quietly I said, " Well, I don't."

Shoshy realized her mistake and was very embarrassed. Quickly, she said, "Oh, Raizel, I'm so sorry." Then we went off to do our homework.

Her response was perfect — short, but sweet.

Note: Now I wish I had told those other girls to appreciate their fathers and not to mock someone who does.

Sad

Whenever I got upset about something small, everyone always assumed it had something to do with the fact that I had no father. I know exactly what they thought: "This is her way of letting her tears out, by crying over something unimportant." And they were right.

Maybe something connected to Tatti had bothered me a week before, but I couldn't let it out, and then, when someone took my toy, I, a third-grader, would cry. All the pain and hurt inside me would build up and when it reached a certain point, I would explode.

Please be more sensitive to someone like me! Let us cry even if it's about a small, silly thing. When my brother would cry, I hated hearing people say to him, "Come on, you have to be a man now!" When men lose their fathers, don't they cry?

Tatti Is Still with Us

I still remember Tatti. Sometimes something happens and I think, Tatti would like this. I wish he were here.

Our cousin came from Israel, and one Shabbos she told us different stories about Tatti and his brothers. We were all laughing and I couldn't help thinking how Tatti would have liked this.

Time goes on and our wounds heal, but we are still left with a scar. I never forget that I don't have a father, because how can I? But I don't have to forget him to move on. I just had to learn to live without him physically, because... he will always be in my heart.

*   *   *

TEENAGERS IN MOURNING

Teenagers often find the required year of mourning for their parent to be a difficult and restrictive one. It is advisable for a parent to consult a Rabbi throughout this year concerning what his teenager may and may not do, since some of his answers could depend on how the child is emotionally coping with the situation.

Below, several teenagers' experiences are described. They reveal their very individual thoughts and feelings during this turbulent time. Whatever activities they participated in or refrained from were in accordance with their Rabbi's advice.

The years between ages 12 and 18 are ones of upheaval for both boys and girls. They must cope with physical changes, mood swings, and the persistent desire to figure out who they are in relation to those around them. This is a natural process, and given the opportunity to establish their identities in a secure, stable, and loving environment under the tactful and caring supervision of their parents, they will mature into emotionally healthy adults.

Yet, imagine having to go through the turmoil of the teenage years — asking yourself exactly who you are and what you believe in — and then having to deal with the loss of a parent and a year of mourning as well. (The pressure can be compounded when a girl loses her mother or a boy his father.) Just when they are beginning to make their way through this new, exciting stage in their development, everything around them seems to change in a surreal way.

One thing that helps them get through their early stage of grieving is to gently encourage them in the course of a natural conversation or activity to express their feelings and relive their memories of their parent who died. But they should be the ones to bring up the subject. Do not just happen to "casually" lead a discussion in that direction.

Do not stifle anything your children have to say, even if it makes you feel uncomfortable. In most cases, they do not want to forget about their deceased parent, even though losing him/her was the greatest tragedy they have ever suffered.

(There are instances where such children on their wedding day made an effort to include their deceased parent in their *simchah*. Based upon ancient kabbalistic teachings, a bride or a groom who has lost a parent might very discreetly light a *yahrtzeit* candle under the wedding canopy. This is done as a means of "inviting that parent" to share the *simchah* with him/her. The custom of lighting *yahrtzeit* candles in general is derived from the verse, "The soul of a man is the lamp of Hashem" [*Mishlei* 20:27].)

Teenagers should be reassured that their need to grieve for their parent (no matter when) is perfectly normal. If you validate their intense sorrow whenever they experience it, they begin to feel comfortable enough to go on with their lives. Then they need you to assure them that there is nothing wrong with feeling happy again.

During this year, teenagers benefit immensely by developing a relationship with their Rabbi. Once they feel comfortable with him, they will not hesitate to call and ask him their many questions, such as: which school and sports activities are they permitted to join, or is there a way they can take part in a friend's or family member's celebration. It is better for them to ask such questions, rather than to assume that they can't go anywhere or do anything. If a teenager does not feel comfortable calling his Rabbi every time he has a question, his parent should take the initiative and do it for him.

One widow said the following:

> After my husband died, our Rabbi spoke personally with each of my children. He told them that the purpose of the year of mourning is not to be in pain and to cry all the time, but, instead, to give them the opportunity to honor their father, even though he was no longer around. He explained that this would be their last gift to their father. This warm and comforting explanation really helped my kids.

One teenage girl listed the things that were most difficult for her during her year of mourning: not wearing new clothes each Yom Tov like her classmates, not attending her favorite teacher's engagement celebration, sitting and eating in a hallway with her siblings while everyone else was eating together after the *bris* of a baby who was named after her father, and not attending an out-of-town Shabbaton with her friends.

Teenage boys find the year of mourning hard because they are required to recite *Kaddish* for their parent with a *minyan* three times a day. Even if they sleep at a friend's house for Shabbos, they have to make sure not to miss a *minyan*. As one mother explained, "My sons understood that they were elevating their father's soul every time they said *Kaddish* for him. But, the three-times-a-day reminder that they no longer had a father did not give their wounded hearts much of a chance to heal."

Kaddish is also the reason why some teenage boys prefer not to go to sleepaway camp during the summer, even though it would give them the chance to get away and relax. "It's hard to say *Kaddish* in my own shul, but it's doubly hard to do it in front of the camp counselors, administrators, and campers who don't know about my situation," one boy explained.

What also makes this year difficult for teenagers is that their remaining parent is only required to observe thirty days of mourning. While their parent can resume going to celebrations, buying and wearing new clothes, and listening to music, they still have to wait. This can make things awkward at home during the year.

These teenagers greatly appreciate other people's sensitivity towards them... and so does their remaining parent. They want to give their deceased parent the proper respect that s/he deserves, and at the same time, they derive comfort from doing so. Teenagers' meticulous observance of the laws of mourning certainly deserves our highest accolades.

Michael's Story

The year after I lost my mother, someone paid for my brothers and me to go to sleepaway camp. All of us were very excited about going. I was especially happy, since my best friend was going to that camp, too.

The first week, I enjoyed myself. But on Shabbos, during the late afternoon meal, I suddenly became very homesick for my father and started to miss my mother very much. The songs that everyone was singing, with their moving words and beautiful melodies, were touching me deeply and making me feel sad. I couldn't sit there anymore, so I left the room.

I didn't want anyone to see me crying, so I made a beeline for my bunk, which was (fortunately) empty. I just plunged my head into my pillow and cried. A few minutes later my counselor came into the room. I knew that the counselors had been informed of my situation, so when my counselor asked me what was the matter, I told him the truth: that sometimes I really missed my mother.

His answer was, "You know, Michael, you should just appreciate the father that you have and not dwell on the fact that you don't have a mother. Why, I'll bet there are kids that don't have either a father or a mother!" I was so taken aback by his insensitive words that I have never forgotten them!

Nava's Story

When I was a senior in high school, I lost my mother. Even though she had been sick for a long time, it was still a terrible blow. I felt so at a loss and disconnected to everyone around me. And then, at school it was time to plan the senior concert to present to the community. It's the highlight of the school year. All the girls take part — either in the choir, the dance, the ensemble, or the play. The school was just abuzz with all of the planning and rehearsing.

I cannot begin to describe how terrible it was for me not to be able to take part in it. I have a pretty nice voice and usually I get a solo. I couldn't stop thinking that after all I went through that year, I wasn't going to be able to join in something that gave me so much pleasure. (I didn't want to sew costumes and I didn't have the enthusiasm to sell tickets to the performance.) All of my friends were either staying late at school or getting together at someone else's house to practice for weeks on end, so I felt incredibly alone.

The night of the performance, a few of my friends dropped by with donuts and balloons to tell me that they would really miss me. It was such a nice and thoughtful gesture. Yet when the clock struck eight and I knew the choir was starting without me, I just sobbed into my pillow.

Leora's Story

The whole school was going ice-skating at a huge rink that our student council had rented out. I am not such a good ice skater, but still I was disappointed that I had to miss a big social event. Since they were supposed to go that afternoon, I didn't feel like going to school that morning and my mother let me stay home.

Around lunchtime there was a knock at our front door. When I went to open it, there stood two of my friends. They said that they didn't like to skate, so they had come over to spend the afternoon with me. I felt bad that they hadn't gone (I'm not sure their story was true), but it made me feel so good that they came to be with me. We worked on a school project together and then went out for ice cream. To this day I remember how happy they made me feel!

Paying a Shivah Call to a Child or Teenager

Classmates and teachers should know how to pay a *Shivah* call and what to expect:

▶ When a teenager loses a parent, a professional should speak to his class about what they will see in the mourner's house when they go. They also should be given instructions on how to behave, since it might be the first time that they have ever paid a *Shivah* call. It helps them to be forewarned that some houses are very quiet while others are bustling with activity.

▶ Classmates can visit individually with their parents or together in small groups at different times throughout the week. (Many schools make the arrangements for this.) Boys over Bar Mitzvah age usually go to pray in the *minyan* at the mourner's house and then stay to pay a *Shivah* call.

▶ Teenagers really look forward to having their friends come and spend time with them when they sit *Shivah*. They especially appreciate their closest friends coming during the evening hours, when the house tends to fill up with adults.

▶ Young children can "sit *Shivah*," but they really are not yet obligated. They like when their friends and classmates come over. As hard as it might be for a young child to enter a *Shivah* house, it can be a great learning experience for him and he will be less hesitant to do it again in the future. (If some parents think that their children are too young to pay a *Shivah* call, the class as a whole can write their classmate individual letters or make a huge poster-board card for him filled with "I Miss You" messages.)

▶ Friends who are planning to make a *Shivah* call should be told that the young mourner might not be feeling like himself. He could be despondent, extremely weepy, very withdrawn, or even overly demonstrative. They should be told that this is considered normal for people who have suffered a great personal loss. They should overlook the change and let their friend know how terribly sorry they are about his/her loss.

▶ Teenagers said they felt a little embarrassed when their teachers came to see them, but deep down, they were flattered that they had bothered.

Example: One teenager said that during *Shivah*, one of her teachers had given her a blank journal with a note attached, telling her to write down her memories of her deceased parent. Whenever things quieted down in the *Shivah* house, she made use of it. Years later, whenever she looks at what she wrote that week, she thinks fondly of the teacher who had the sensitivity and insight to buy that journal for her.

Example: Shimon was fifteen when he lost his father. Even though his father had been ill for many years, he was still devastated. When the family came home after the funeral, he went straight to his room and could not be persuaded by his mother or anyone else to come out and eat the traditional mourners' first meal of hard-boiled eggs. He just lay on his bed, staring at the ceiling.

A few hours later, Shimon's good friend Nesanel came over to see how he was doing. After being told where Shimon was, he quietly knocked on his bedroom door and entered. The boys stayed in there for a few hours before Shimon rejoined his family to sit *Shivah* in the living room.

When Shimon's mother saw Nesanel a few weeks later in the grocery store, she thanked him for being there for Shimon that day. He told her the following, "I just went in and lay down on the other bed and stared at the ceiling along with him. After about an hour Shimon started talking about everything — and I didn't say anything. I just let him talk." Sometimes, just quietly keeping someone company is what's really needed.

WHAT YOU CAN DO FOR OUR DAUGHTERS AND OUR SONS

With so many adverse, "outside" influences permeating everyday life, children who have lost parents or who have someone seriously ill or disabled at home are particularly susceptible to them — especially if they are not getting the proper attention and guidance that they need as a result of the situation.

Taking these children under your arm is a wonderful thing to do. But, it is also important to spend quiet, quality time with your own children. If your child really needs your undivided attention, you are not helping anyone by inviting another child to join the two of you. However, if your relationship with your own child is good, then inviting another child along is one of the best things you can do. For one thing, it will teach your children to care for and have concern for others who are going through a difficult time.

Don't Forget About Our Daughters

A motherless girl can benefit from a close relationship with a teacher, a friend's mother or older sister, a neighbor, an aunt, or a cousin — anyone responsible who is warm and loving towards her. It is very important for a young girl to build good, solid relationships with women and teenagers who can be a positive influence on her and who she will want to emulate.

A girl who has lost her mother needs an older woman to be her friend and perhaps even her role model. Try to include such a girl in your plans occasionally. If you make a weekly or monthly commitment to her, be sure to stick with it. Those times will mean the world to this girl, and the time she spends together with you might honestly be the highlight of her week.

A problem might arise if the child feels that someone is trying to usurp her mother's place in her life. This is a fine line to walk, so tread carefully! Rather than pushing yourself into a girl's life, gradually get closer before you try to guide her. Even though it is a great responsibility, a woman can reap wonderful rewards for taking one of these girls into her home — and her heart!

This can be done in any of the following ways:

▶ Invite her over when you are cooking and baking for Shabbos or Yom Tov to help you and to be your "favorite taste-tester!"

▶ Invite her along to keep you company whenever you have to go to the shopping mall or the supermarket.

▶ If you are a youth group leader, ask her to help you.

▶ Include her in a game of volleyball, tennis, or to come along on a boat ride.

▶ Take her to a botanical garden.

- ▶ Offer to tutor her in any subject she needs.
- ▶ If you are a teacher, ask her to help you set up your classroom for the coming year or to make a project.
- ▶ If your line of work interests her, invite her to come to work with you sometimes or get her a job in your office during summer vacation.
- ▶ Offer to drive her to whatever exercise activity she chooses, i.e., dancing, skating, sports.
- ▶ If you enjoy doing needlepoint and she wants to learn, go with her to a crafts store and pick out a kit that you can help her with.
- ▶ Take her to a museum appropriate for her age and interests.
- ▶ Go berry picking on a farm and come back and make fresh blueberry pies!
- ▶ Take her along when you go to a "For Women Only" performance.

Example: Suzanna was going through a very hard time. The previous year, at the age of fourteen, she had lost her mother. Family and friends tried their best to be there for her, but she was withdrawing more and more into herself and becoming a very lonely child.

A neighbor suggested to her father that he enroll Suzanna in a Big Sister program sponsored by their local Jewish Family Services, where women volunteer their time to take a girl who needs a little extra attention to the zoo, or bowling, or some other fun place that donates free admission tickets.

Suzanna, of course, was adamant against joining, but she agreed to try it to appease her father. When he called the director of the program, he explained about his daughter and warned that they would have only one chance to make this work.

A few months later the director called to tell him that she had not forgotten about Suzanna at all. Rather she had just been waiting for the "perfect match" to volunteer, and finally she had.

The next week, Molly came into Suzanna's life, and the director of the program was absolutely right on the mark! Molly became the big sister that Suzanna needed, and Suzanna's whole attitude took a turn for the better as they became close.

Don't Forget About Our Sons

A boy needs a male role model if there is no father in the picture. He should be someone that the child can respect and feel comfortable talking to about anything. Unfortunately, fewer men than women get involved in this sort of thing. But when these special individuals do take an active role, it can mean all the difference in the world to a fatherless boy.

Younger boys will automatically reach out to someone who shows them genuine warmth and concern and who is fun to be with, too. But he might feel resentful if he thinks someone is trying to replace his father. Teenage boys generally form a close relationship with a Rebbe, Rav, uncle, cousin, or a friend's father.

If a fatherless boy or teenager tries to become close to you, take it as a great compliment. It is so important to set aside some time on a regular basis to be with him. Everyone has busy lives with hectic schedules, but it is not all that difficult to walk back and forth to synagogue with a boy, or to sit next to him in synagogue on Shabbos and guide him in the services. (Many widows noted that what their teenage sons missed most was not being able to do this with their father, but they would not agree to do this with another man unless they felt very comfortable with him.)

If your weekday or Sunday schedule is overloaded, make sure to call your teenage friend once a week just to ask how he is doing. This telephone gesture is greatly appreciated. Then whenever you possibly can, take him out to run errands with you or to chat whenever you are working on a special project/hobby. By keeping you company, he can gain a world of knowledge from hearing what you think and watching what you do.

You can help a fatherless boy in any of the following ways:

- ▶ Take him to play baseball, basketball, football, or soccer. Ball games are very important to boys and it is a healthy outlet that should be encouraged. Of course, the ultimate good time is to take a boy to a professional ball game — especially at night!
- ▶ Take him swimming. It is a healthy way for him to release his pent-up energy.
- ▶ Take him to a car show. Boys love looking at antique cars or the latest models. The same goes for a boat show.
- ▶ Take him to a park or some outdoor area that he can explore. He can bring his bicycle along and ride on the bike trails, or he can climb some rocks.
- ▶ If there's a citizens' patrol in your town, take him with you in the patrol car so he can hear the announcements over the police channel.
- ▶ Take him to your office for a day or get him a summer job where you work.
- ▶ Study Torah with him alone or invite him to join you and your son at father/son learning groups.
- ▶ If you are a youth group leader, ask him to help you plan an activity or set up.
- ▶ Offer to tutor him in whatever subject he needs.
- ▶ Include him in a camping trip, something that all boys enjoy. They love learning how to pitch tents, make a campfire, cook, etc.

(Check the "Don't Forget About Our Daughters" section, which immediately precedes this one, for more ideas.)

Example: Mrs. Pearson was a widow who was left with two sons. When one of them reached the eighth grade and it was time to start applying to yeshivos for high school, a Rebbe in the community took it upon himself to look into the schools for this boy and to take him for entrance exams. Even if the yeshiva was located several hours away and it took this Rebbe the entire day, he went without a moment's hesitation. (He also had his wife's full support in doing this.) Mrs. Pearson was very grateful for his help because she didn't know which yeshiva would be best for her son.

On a Personal Note: The men who made it their business to study Torah with my sons or to take them out were all busy people, very involved in their shul, with jobs that required a tremendous amount of responsibility, and were active on either a school board or in a Jewish organization in our town — not to mention their own family commitments. Yet all of them took the time to make a connection with my sons. As the saying goes: "If you want something done, ask a busy person."

Example: Rosalyn's son, Eric, was going through a particularly hard time since his parents' divorce. His father had moved out of town and they saw each other only every other weekend.

Rosalyn spoke with a friend of hers, who suggested that she get Eric involved in some project he would enjoy. So Rosalyn called a friend of hers, Jack Berger, who was an engineer. Rosalyn knew that Jack was currently adding a bedroom to his house.

Even though Jack was very busy supervising the workmen and ordering the supplies, he graciously suggested that Eric come and help him for a few hours a week. As it turned out, Eric enjoyed working there so much that he convinced his best friend to come and help them, too.

Jack always extended a warm greeting to Eric and made him feel welcome. He gave Eric things to work on and taught him as he went along. It really helped boost Eric's morale.

Example: Janet was widowed and left with two teenage boys and several younger children. She told me the following:

> I told my son that maybe he should *daven* in a different shul, now that he had lost his father, but he wanted to stay where he was because all of his friends came to this one. It so happened that I went to hear a speaker at that shul one week, and when I glanced into where my son's *minyan* was holding a father-son learning session between the afternoon and evening prayers, I was totally shocked! Every boy was learning together with his father or older brother, while my son was left sitting all alone! I tell you, when I saw that, it destroyed me.
>
> That evening I asked my son about it and he told me that he felt funny asking one of his friends' fathers if he could join them. Now, these men all knew that my son had lost his father. I had just assumed that one of them would take it upon himself to include my son. With a heavy heart I telephoned and arranged for my son to join a friend and his father the following week, and I never assumed anything else again!

On a Personal Note: Years ago, before Dovid became ill, someone approached him and asked if he could learn a few times a week with a boy from a divorced home. We didn't know the family well, but Dovid decided to give it a try.

Since the boy was young and couldn't stay out late, he usually arrived as soon as Dovid came home from work — around the children's bath time. It was a little inconvenient for us, but we did it.

Then, as Dovid's job required him to travel more and he missed more and more sessions with this boy, he had to tell the boy's mother, Chaviva, that he just couldn't be counted on to learn with her son anymore.

I saw the sorrowful look in her eyes, but she didn't say a word other than to graciously thank Dovid for the time he had spent with her son. (The truth was, Dovid could have learned with him on Shabbos or Sunday, or we could have invited them over for a Shabbos meal, but not understanding what they were going through, we just didn't think about it.)

Years passed and suddenly I found myself confronted with the situation of being both a mother and a father to my sons. One night, after making a phone call to ask someone if he could accompany my son to a father-son activity, I experienced a very clear flashback. Once again I saw Chaviva's face when we told her she would have to find someone else to learn with her son.

Now, I realized, I knew EXACTLY what she had been feeling then. I bitterly, bitterly regret not trying to do more for them. However, I must add that whenever I see Chaviva, she always greets me with a smile. To my great relief, she never, ever held a grudge against us.

On Another Personal Note: My oldest son, Moshe, was asked to write an end-of-the-year paragraph in school on any subject of his choosing. Even though his father had died seven years earlier, he chose to express his thankfulness to the men who had helped over the years.

My Father, by Moshe Feldbaum

A sad time in my life was when my father died. I would see other people walking around with their fathers and it made me feel sad that I don't have one. My friends' fathers came to me and cheered me up. They walked me to shul and back. They cared for me like a father. They taught me how to *duchin* and say *Kiddush* every Shabbos night. Another man does homework with me every night. They managed to help me because I don't have a father.

Chapter Eight:

You Get More Out of Life When You Stop and Smell the Roses

I learned a great deal about life at the ripe old age of thirty-seven, when I became a widow and a single parent. I felt overwhelmed by all of the mammoth responsibilities that now were mine. The seeming enormity of everything was blocking my ability to see clearly. But over time I learned the following:

- ▶ Life goes on, no matter how enormous the loss.
- ▶ Once you have fallen into the depths of an abyss, you cannot clearly recognize all the good that is still in your life.
- ▶ There is always a light at the end of the tunnel, even though it looks so far away.

I was once complaining about how difficult everything had become for me to a woman who was widowed in her 50s and yet always managed to keep up a cheerful demeanor. I had nothing but respect for her. To this she replied, "You know, Becca, as much as I miss my husband, I know that everything that Hashem does is for the best. And I really believe that! Only... I wish that He would ask me for my opinion every once in a while!" That really made me laugh.

Upon deeper reflection, I understood that what she was trying to tell me was: If I wanted to cope with all of my challenges, I was going to have to internalize this basic tenet of Judaism — everything Hashem does is for the best. It was my task to look for the good in everything and to be grateful for it, instead of feeling sorry for myself all day long.

And so, I began thanking Hashem... quietly, just for the small things. I said thank You whenever I kissed my kids to wake them up, whenever they played together nicely, whenever I finished doing an errand, whenever I was able to lie down for a few minutes and rest, whenever I was invited out for a Shabbos meal, whenever the weather was nice and I could take the kids outdoors, whenever a friend called, etc.

Doing this forced me to "stop and smell the roses" — to look around and see all the good and beautiful things in my life instead of focusing on what was missing. It also led me to take more time to appreciate all the blessings that Hashem has given me. Instead of spiraling downward in depression, it helped me to see everything in a better perspective and made me into a much more positive person.

Epilogue

A GOOD FRIEND OF MINE, Sarah, had a neighbor, Kayla, whose husband had died. Kayla's story was similar to mine — she was a young widow with small children. Kayla's family and friends rallied around her, yet she still felt desolate.

Almost a month after Kayla's husband died, Sarah saw her outside in her garden one day and went over to ask her how she was doing and whether she could help her with anything. Kayla answered Sarah's question by talking non-stop about how hard her life was now: she was lonely, she was worried about money, she was concerned that she would not be a good single parent, and she felt devastated over losing her husband.

These women were not close. They had only exchanged neighborly waves whenever they saw each other, and occasionally their children had played together outside. They led very different lifestyles and did not have much in common. My friend was taken aback that Kayla had unleashed so many of her private thoughts and worries. But Sarah did not assume that she was expected to say anything or to offer her opinion. Instead, she just stood quietly and listened, wearing a sympathetic expression on her face.

A few weeks later Kayla called Sarah. She apologized for her outburst that day and told Sarah that she was so happy that Sarah hadn't offered her any advice, but had just stood there and calmly listened to her. She wanted Sarah to know that she was doing much better and that she appreciated her "being there for her" and letting her vent her anger, fears, and frustrations.

Afterwards Sarah immediately picked up the phone and called me. This is basically what she said.

> Becca, from the discussions I have had with you, I understood that Kayla was not really complaining that her life was so terrible, but she was having a hard day coping with her loss and this was how she was expressing it. If you and I had never spoken about this before, I probably would have interrupted her and insisted, "Oh, life isn't so bad. Try not to focus on your tragedy and just focus on your beautiful children instead." But really, that would have been so insensitive. Here I am with a healthy family — a wonderful husband, three great kids, and no real financial worries. There is no way I can relate to her pain and sorrow on a personal level. But I learned from talking with you how best to deal with this kind of situation and I just listened. That was all she really needed.

That phone call gave me the incentive to finish this book. I saw that, through my example, I was teaching people around me how to understand and to help others who were going through a painful situation. If this book teaches even one reader to be sensitive and to thereby spare another person from a minute's weeping, then I have achieved my goal.

Appendices

Appendix One:

What Patients and Their Families Would Love to Say to Doctors

1. Please do not "jumble up" all of your sick patients. Keep in mind that they are all individuals with family and friends who love and care about them.

2. Once you perform the initial tests to determine why a person is not feeling well, it is agony for him/her to wait for the results. No matter how busy your schedule is, try to let him/her know as soon as you've evaluated the data.

3. If the tests results are not good, be open and honest with the family members on the day that you tell them, but do not go into all the gory details about what will happen to the person or how the medicines will make him feel. They need time to absorb the shock of the bad news first; they will not be able to concentrate on anything else. Schedule a separate meeting about the treatments available.

4. Whenever you walk into the patient's hospital room, keep in mind that the family members may have been waiting hours just to speak with you for a few minutes. Try to answer all of their questions as clearly as you can and in layman's terms.

5. Before an adult or a child is released from the hospital, clear instructions need to be given to their caregivers. If you do not have the time to carefully go over the instructions before the patient is released, make sure that a qualified medical student, nurse, or nurse practitioner will thoroughly explain how to take care of the patient at home and which signs of declining health to be on the lookout for.

Whoever is dispensing this essential information should not rush through it a few minutes before the patient is released from the hospital. Everything should be explained as patiently as possible and the caregivers should be allowed plenty of time to ask as many questions as they want. Also, it is difficult for someone not familiar with medical jargon to completely understand certain instructions if they are not explained in layman's terms.

Caring for a family member at home can be frightening for someone not in the medical field. Therefore there should be some daily form of communication between the doctor's office and the caregiver until she feels completely comfortable with her new responsibilities.

6. Listen carefully to what your patients tell you. People don't always feel exactly the way the medical books say they should. Doctors and surgeons who take their patients' words seriously can diagnose the medical problem faster. Doctors also need to address their patient's unspoken fears. This is what makes the difference between an average and an exceptional doctor.

Example: "When my wife and I chose doctors for our daughter, how they spoke to us did not matter as much as how they interacted with her. We were extremely lucky to find a warm and caring pediatrician and children's neurologist who treated our daughter with the greatest of respect. They held her hand while they were conferring with us and they were very careful about how they spoke about her while she was still in the room. Those small, kind gestures mattered so much to us while we were going through this extremely difficult time."

What Doctors Would Love to Say to Patients and Their Families

1. Keep in mind that a doctor is only God's messenger.

2. Please arrive on time for your scheduled appointments. You should come prepared with a list of all the questions and concerns that you want to discuss with the physician.

3. Bring all your bottles of medicine, full and empty, whenever you have a doctor's appointment. That way the doctor can check that the patient is taking the correct medicine in the right amounts. Don't blame the doctor if you are not feeling well because you did not take your medicine properly or you delayed going for the tests he ordered.

4. When someone is sick, just one family member should be appointed to deal with the doctor. This is much more efficient — the doctor will not receive conflicting reports or requests and will not have to make repeated phone calls to different family members. Crucial information will be transmitted to one person only, and this person will then relay everything to the rest of the family regarding the patient's treatment and progress.

5. Be open with the doctor regarding all of your problems and fears. That is the only way he will be able to diagnose all of your symptoms and treat you properly. It is also very important to let him know how you are handling your illness emotionally. As one doctor said, "Lawsuits often arise out of poor communication — not poor medicine!"

6. No doctor should mind if you go for a second opinion. But discuss this with your physician first so that he can write

out a report about your care. And, when you do go for another opinion, do not forget to bring all of your old medical records and bottles of medicine.

7. Good doctor/patient relationships should not spill over into a doctor's personal, private time (i.e., at a social gathering), unless it is urgent. As one doctor said, "I don't mind being bothered by those who don't want to bother me; those who don't care make my life difficult."

Appendix Three:

Expect the Best, But Prepare for the Worst

CAROL WAVED GOODBYE to her husband, Saul, as he left for work one morning, not realizing that she would never see him alive again.

After lunch that day, he suffered a fatal heart attack at his desk. His coworkers tried valiantly to revive him, but by the time the ambulance arrived, he had died.

Carol said that she could not believe what had happened to her husband. It was all so sudden. She was in a daze for weeks.

It is particularly sad when tragedy strikes and a couple is totally unprepared. Many husbands and wives never take the time to put their affairs in order, should one or both of them die. Even if they do not have much in the way of savings or do not own any property, a legal will is essential in order to ensure who will inherit what little they have. Also, it is imperative for them to put in writing whom they would like to raise their children if, God forbid, anything should happen to them. (If, for some reason, you and your spouse cannot bring yourselves to do this with a lawyer, then write down all the information on a sheet of paper, have it notarized, and put it away in a safe place, i.e., a fire-proof box at home, a locked box in your office, or a safety deposit box at your bank.)

As a final important note, be sure that you have a good life insurance policy. Most people are careful about purchasing insurance coverage for their home and their car, but they somehow underrate the need for life insurance. It should be considered an essential investment for the spouse's and children's future. A life insurance policy is much less risky than investing in the stock market because it has a guaranteed payout. Also, should something happen to you, your spouse and children will have some money to keep them financially viable for awhile and they will not have to become a financial burden on their community. (When a couple asked a well-known Rabbi whether they should buy a life insurance policy, his reply was that it was completely irresponsible for them not to have one!)

With all the pain and sorrow that accompanies a death, who needs the incredible burden of financial problems as well? If you don't do it for yourself, then please do it for your family's sake.

Example: One couple who became grandparents for the first time gave their daughter and son-in-law, for a baby gift, a blank will and enough money to pay for the first year of a life insurance policy! The grandparents told them that now that they had taken on the responsibility of raising a child, they had to give him some financial security.

Example: In a certain city, an unusual number of young husbands passed away over the course of two years. In response, the Jewish community took up a collection to provide for the widows and children.

A local philanthropist noticed that it was becoming a great burden on the community to raise the necessary sums. In order to prevent this from happening again in the future, he decided to set up a $1,000,000 trust fund that would pay for $250,000-life-insurance policies for all of the men who had received rabbinical ordination who taught in the Jewish schools in his town. He saw that many of them had large families and might not understand how important it was to buy life insurance when they had other more immediate expenses at home. He helped these families in the best way possible through his generosity and keen insight.

Acknowledgments

It is so hard for me to truly express my complete heartfelt thanks to my family members and my friends who have stood by my side and helped me out all of these years but... I will certainly try!

How can I even try to thank *HaKadosh Baruch Hu* for all that He has done for me and given me? I am eternally grateful to Him for so many things but, most importantly, having been raised by such wonderful parents, having the good fortune to be married to a kind and thoughtful husband, and being blessed with my four children, Raizel, Chaya Gittel, Moshe, and Michoel Simcha. I am so thankful for all of the *berachos HaKadosh Baruch Hu* has showered on my family and I pray that He will continue to do so throughout our lives. I sincerely hope that my readers will take my advice in the "You Get More Out of Life When You Stop and Smell the Roses" part of this book. It can truly make a profound difference in your life.

I want to give my most heartfelt *hakaras ha-tov* to Connie and Avi Lazar for all that they have done for me and my children throughout the years. Connie and Avi were one of a very small "elite" group of friends and close relatives who knew about Dovid's condition from the very beginning. When we were going through so many difficult times when Dovid was ill, they were vigilant in doing whatever they could for my husband and our family to make our lives a little bit easier. Yet, instead of gradually ebbing away from us and going on to lead their own lives after he passed away, they have steadfastly stuck by me and have truly played an important, central role in my life. Since the *petirah* of my husband, Avi has been there for my sons, readily taking them to the synagogue on Shabbos or the Yom Tovim, or volunteering to go with them to any father–son activity they want to participate in, or including them in anything that he does with his own sons. This, obviously, has been a tremendous help to me and greatly appreciated. And, no matter how busy Connie is, she has always made the time to help me over any difficult hurdle I encounter, coming over as soon as she can whenever I need her. It has truly meant a great deal to me knowing I have a friend who realizes that I do not necessarily need her spoken advice but I just may need to speak things out with someone to clarify for myself how to handle certain challenging or emotional situations. Believe me, as a single parent, to have a friendship like this is truly priceless. In the *zechus* of all that they have done for me and my family, I want to wish this very special couple only *nachas* from their wonderful children: Daniel, Chaya, Esti, Mordechai, Elchonon, and Sara Baila.

My brother and sister-in-law, Dr. Harris and Hadar Bram, have opened up their home to my children and myself every Sukkos and Pesach since my husband passed away. It helped me out so much to spend this time with them and not have to worry about these Yom Tovim preparations, especially in the first years of my widowhood when my children were very young and it was an extremely hard, emotional time for me. I am especially appreciative of Hadar, who always made my family feel so wanted and comfortable in their home and of Harris who flew with me and my daughters to Israel when I lost my husband so I would not have to watch them alone on that endlessly long and sad airplane flight. In the *zechus* of the wonderful *gemillas chasadim* that Harris and Hadar have shown to so many people in all the cities where they have lived (Little Rock, AR, Philadelphia, PA, Elberon, NJ, and now in East Brunswick, NJ) I hope that they will only get much *nachas* in the future years from their children, my nieces and nephews, Ariella Shifra, Yehudit Davida, Aliza Batya, Gavriel Tzvi, and Yosef Shimshon.

Mary Zinstein, who was my roommate at Touro College, and Pepi Cohen, who was my roommate at Neve Yerushalayim, are more like sisters to me than friends. Throughout these past years, Mary and Pepi have steadfastly stood by me through the good times and the bad. I truly feel that Mary is my anchor, as she is an incredibly wonderful sounding board to speak to about any situations that come up where I have to make a major decision alone. And Pepi is my ray of sunshine, because whenever I am down about something or feel lonely, she is always there to lift my spirits with her smiling, ever-so-cheerful demeanor. Their husbands, Yitzchok Zinstein and Jeffrey Cohen, have also made every effort to be there for my children and myself and always make us feel extremely welcome in their homes. I feel incredibly fortunate that "by the luck of the draw," these women were my roommates and to this day are two of my closest friends.

My daughter, Chaya Gittel, was a tremendous source of help to me while I was writing this book. Chaya Gittel read everything I wrote many times over and gave me her youthful insights which, I feel, really added a lot to any point I wanted to make. I especially want to thank her for the back massages she would give me in the evenings when I had spent practically the entire day typing at the computer and my muscles were really aching! Out of everything, I appreciated that the most! I also want to thank my daughter, Raizel, for writing the section in the children's chapter, "Raizel's Story." I am greatly indebted to her for sharing with us her innermost feelings on how it feels to lose a parent at such a young age which, I am sure, will be a real eye-opener for anyone who reads it.

The true backbone of this book comes from a very, very special Rebbetzin, Rebbetzin Chana Weinberg, daughter of R. Yaakov Yitzchok Ruderman (*a"h*) and wife of R. Shmuel Yaakov Weinberg (*a"h*). Since the inception of this book, Rebbetzin Weinberg has taking an interest in everything involved with it. One of the nicest times I can ever remember having with her was the two hours I spent on her porch one beautiful spring day where she read over my manuscript as I sat next to her, pen poised in my hand with my notebook on my lap, waiting to hear her thoughts and ideas. As the head of the Bikkur Cholim organization in Baltimore, MD for many years, Rebbetzin Weinberg was extremely helpful in giving me the information I needed for that section of my book. May *HaKadosh Baruch Hu* give her the strength to continue to do her wonderful work with Bikkur Cholim, not only in Baltimore, but throughout the world.

I started taking daily therapeutic walks in the morning when my husband became ill and I continue to do so to this day. A few times a week I walk with my walking partners, Ilana Smith and Dina Cotton. When I was in the final stages of finishing this book, many times Ilana and Dina listened to my book ideas the entire time we walked and never, ever did either one ever say to me, "Becca, enough already!" For their patience and friendship, I am so grateful.

The words "thank you" do not adequately describe how much it has meant to me to have friends who are *always there for me*. From the bottom of my heart, I want to thank my Baltimore *chevrah*, Chava Drebin, Cheryl Greenfield, Shoshana Kruger, Malka Levine, Chasia Menchel, and Judy Zapinsky for...EVERYTHING! I am also so grateful to my friends who live out-of-town, who keep in touch with me to see how the kids and I are doing, especially around the time of the Yom Tovim; Rona Holzer (Miami Beach, FL), Elisheva Botwinick (Monsey, NY), Ida Soberman (Toronto, Canada), Michal Apelbaum, Geula Preil, and Ella Katz (Jerusalem, Israel). And last, but certainly not least, a very, very special thank you is in order to Dina Blaustein, our family's very own Tante D, who truly exemplifies what it means to be a *ba'alas chesed*... and a good friend.

When my husband became ill, Miriam Robbins was the first *almanáh* who called me on the phone and offered to help me out in any way possible. I have learned so much from her over the years on how to truly help people going through difficult situations, especially in knowing what to do for a widow who has recently lost her husband. I feel incredibly fortunate to be friends with Miriam since her sincere attitude that "everything Hashem does is for the best" has had a great influence on me and helped me get through many difficult times. I truly value and cherish our friendship.

Through the years, I became extremely closely connected with three other women who had also, unfortunately, lost their beloved spouses: Miriam (Weiss) Blumenkrantz, Rochel Mandelbaum, and Gloria Feldman. We try to be there for each other, sharing our *simchahs* together and being a strong support system for one another when family situations get rough at times. To this day, my friendships with all four of these wonderful women continue to flourish.

My husband's doctor, Dr. Yoel Jakobovits, was a tremendous source of strength and comfort to both my husband and myself. In the last few months of my husband's life, when Dovid was critically ill, "Dr. J." called our home every *erev Shabbos* to wish us a "Good Shabbos" and to ask how *I* was doing. Those phone calls meant so much to me. Dr. J. taught me how to truly be there for others in their time of need.

I would also like to thank R. Yaakov Hopfer and R. Yakov Horowitz, who gave me *haskamahs* for this book. R. Yaakov Hopfer, our Rav in Baltimore, Maryland is someone whom my husband really respected. R. Hopfer always makes the time to discuss with me any issues I have concerning the spiritual welfare of my children and he does so with real concern and caring about our situation. I am so grateful for all of his guidance over the years. I made the acquaintance of R. Yakov Horowitz when I asked his permission to reprint a paragraph he had written on *yesomim* for this book. Not only did R. Horowitz graciously agree, but he took a real interest in the subject matter of my book because, unfortunately, he lost his own father at a young age. I am extremely grateful for all of his encouragement in writing this book.

Jonah and Rebekka Ottensoser and Bernie and Chana Steinharter are two sisters and their husbands, who have helped me out so much over the years. Rebekka and Chana were one of the very first women to send over their teenage daughters to assist me with my young children after Dovid passed away and, to this day, they keep in touch with me, always making themselves available if I need help or guidance on anything. Mr.

Ottensoser has been learning with my oldest son for years while Mr. Steinharter never misses an opportunity to take my sons out with his son to any activity he thinks they will enjoy. Our lives have become so intertwined with theirs and their children, grandchildren, nieces and nephews, that my children and I really feel like we are part of their families. I also want to give a very special thank you to Rebekka for reading my constant revisions of this book over and over again, giving me her insightful comments and encouraging me to finish writing it.

When I was sitting *Shivah* in Eretz Yisrael for my husband, I got many, many phone calls from friends and family members in Baltimore and all over America. One call that particularly sticks out in my mind was from Nachum and Pnina Eilberg. (Nachum was one of my husband's *chavrusa*s and they had become close friends over the years.) When they spoke with me, Pnina said, "Becca, when you come back to Baltimore, you should just know that Nachum and I will always be here for you and your children." Truer words were never spoken. The Eilbergs' extraordinary caring and kindness towards myself, my parents, and my children has really meant a great deal to me.

Without any hesitation I can honestly say that the person whose guidance helped me the most in the first few years after I lost my husband was Devorah Klein, our grief therapist. There are so many times over the years that I do not know what I would have done without her sage advice. Devorah's care and concern for all of her patients (children and adult alike) always shines through and I particularly admire and respect her straightforward style and the fact that she *really listens* to what a person is saying. Devorah helped me out tremendously when I was writing the chapter on children and I would like to dedicate that chapter to her... one of the finest people I have ever known. I would also like to express my *hakaras ha-tov* to Devorah's husband, my children's pediatrician, Dr. Howard Klein, who initially made the suggestion to me that my children speak with his wife. Dr. Klein has also helped me out with many different, difficult situations that arose over the years and I feel extremely fortunate that my children have a pediatrician who really, truly cares about their physical as well as their emotional well-being.

The "special helpers" that I list here are the teenagers who came to my home for two years or more, either while my husband was ill or after he passed away, to help me with my children. They are: Bayla (Robbins) Barkany, Shira (Schleifer) Cohen, Nachie (Dworkin) Frend, Shifra (Strauss) Gibber, Bruchie (Ottensoser) Mandelbaum, Hindy (Dreyfuss) Kaplan, Miriam (Steinharter) Mansbach, Sara Rivka (Friedman) Moiskowitz,

Shoshana (Strauss) Rogovsky, and Shaindy (Steinharter) Mandelbaum. I am ever so grateful to all of you for the assistance, attention, and love that you gave to my children. I will never forget how much all of you helped me out when I really, really needed it. I dedicate the chapter I wrote on "Things You Can Do to Help on a Regular Weekday" to all of you.

In Baltimore, my husband worked in his profession as a mechanical engineer at Pevco Systems, a company that installs pneumatic tube systems nationwide in office buildings, banks, hospitals, etc. The owner of the company and his sons, Fred Valerino, Sr., Fred Valerino, Jr. and James Valerino bent over backwards to accommodate my husband's needs during his illness, especially in the last few months of his life. From the bottom of my heart I want to thank this family for their extreme kindness to my husband and to let them know that I will never forget how they stood by and supported us at such a difficult time in our lives. I wish them much happiness in their own family lives and success in their company.

My sincere and complete *hakaras ha-tov* also goes to: the Baltimore Jewish community for all that you have done for me and my children over the years; Shearith Israel Congregation for all of the numerous Shabbos and Yom Tov invitations we have gotten from the congregants; Ari and Rochelle Benjamin for the completely unwavering, unbelievable friendship and support that they have shown to my family; Mr. Moshe Goldstein and Mr. Alan Gibber for their "field of expertise" advice that they always graciously give me no matter how busy they are; the warm, caring educational and executive staffs of Bais Yaakov School for Girls of Baltimore and Torah Institute of Baltimore who, many times, bent over backwards to accommodate the needs of my children, especially around the time of the Yom Tovim; Dr. Chaim and Chaviva Dworkin and Rabbi Nosson and Toby Friedman, my neighbors in our "old neighborhood," who went beyond the call of duty to help me out in that incredibly hard first year after my husband passed away; Rabbi Binyomin and Sophia Kohansion, my neighbors in my "new neighborhood," whose home my sons call their "other house on the block"; Elaine Berkowitz, my terrific editor at the *Where, What and When*, who has continually encouraged me over the years to write my humorous articles; Devorah (Weiss) Katz for all of the invaluable, important information and suggestions that she gave me in the children's chapter; Malka Kaganoff who heard about this book years ago and had her daughter, Chaya Baila (Kaganoff) Gavant, type up the first, very basic draft; Sol Levinson and Brothers Funeral Home in Baltimore, Maryland whom I dealt with when my husband passed away and whose professionalism and extreme kindness towards me as a young widow are guidelines which all funeral homes should set their standards by; and a "special individual" who helped guide me on different medical matters during Dovid's illness and to whom I will always be grateful.

I also want to mention some outstanding couples who truly made me feel a part of their families and had a tremendously wonderful influence on me as a teenager and a single young woman. My love, respect, and genuine gratitude for all of them knows no bounds.

There are no words to adequately express my sincere *hakaras ha-tov* to Rabbi Shaya and Nechie Kilimnick, who so inspired my brother and I that it led us to the path of becoming Torah observant Jews. Their tremendous example of *gemillas chasadim* towards their entire congregation, Congregation Agudath Achim in Little Rock, Arkansas ultimately became the springboards for many of the teenagers to lead *shomer Shabbos* lifestyles. The Kilimnicks encouraged Harris to learn in a yeshiva atmosphere after his bar mitzvah and were very instrumental in my involvement in NCSY and subsequently attending Touro College in New York City and Neve Yerushalayim in Jerusalem. To this day I am extremely close with this wonderful couple. And, I do not want to forget to thank Rabbi Seymour and Beverly (*a"h*) Atlas, who instilled in me a love of *Yiddishkeit* at a very young age.

I have had the incredible *zechus* of being considered a *bas bayis* by three very special families in the different cities I have lived in: Rabbi Eliezer and Shulamis Subar in Silver Spring, Maryland (and in Israel), Rabbi Joshua and Miriam Freilich in Bayit Vegan, Jerusalem and Rabbi Berel and Malky Schulman in Toronto, Canada. The standards that I have set for myself and my children on how to live life as a sincere, Torah-true Jew come from the behaviors and actions that I gleaned from all three of these households during the weekdays, Shabbos, and the Yom Tovim. I am still in contact with all three of these families and continue to get a great amount of *chizuk* from them. I also want to mention two other very special couples: Dr. Ronnie and Sara Klompas in Toronto, Canada and Harry (*a"h*) and Rena Klaven in Washington, DC, in whose homes I spent many, many beautiful Shabbosim. And, of course, how can I ever forget the wonderful months I spent with Aunt Hike and Uncle J Schulman, who so warmly opened up their home to me when I got my first job in Washington, DC.

Two of my closest friends from Arkansas, Yocheved Pack and Melanie Rosenberg, made *aliyah* many years ago. Even though thousands of miles separate us, I really feel their concern for me and my children through their phone calls and e-mails. Their sincere dedication to living in Eretz

Yisrael is a constant source of inspiration to me. I am also greatly appreciative of Yocheved's husband, Yossi, and Melanie's husband, Steve, who always made me feel so welcome in their homes. I also want to thank Roz Medlov, a close friend of Melanie's, who originally made the *shidduch* between me and my husband and thought I was worthy enough to marry such a special guy!

I have the great fortune of having been born into a wonderful family on both my mother's side and my father's. My mother's siblings, Molly Klinger (*a"h*), Harmon Tron, Sam Tron, and Roz Weinberg are especially warm, giving, and kind people, and their spouses and children also are blessed with these beautiful *middos*. My uncles and aunts keep in close contact with me and it is such a comforting feeling to know how much they truly love and care about me and my children. My father's siblings, who unfortunately have all passed away, Louis, Mike, Jennie, Reuban Bram, and Gertie (Bram) Kossover, left our family with an unusual legacy. When they were of marriageable age in the Depression years, they did not have the money to pursue a Jewish *shidduch* out of their hometown of Pine Bluff, Arkansas, so none of them (besides my Aunt Gertie who did indeed marry a Jew) married. Having been raised with incredibly strong Jewish values by their parents, they chose to remain single rather than marry out of their faith. I always felt that in their *zechus, HaKadosh Baruch Hu* blessed them by having the next generation of the Bram family, my brother and I, lead religious lifestyles. May all of their great-nieces and great-nephews continue to have their same tenacity when it comes to placing their values in being Jewish above all else.

I certainly do not want to forget the people who made an important impact on my husband, Dovid. Please forgive me if I have inadvertently forgotten anyone.

My husband was fortunate to be able to learn in two outstanding yeshivos in Eretz Yisrael, Shaarei Chaim and Torah Ore, all under the auspices of R. Chaim Pinchas Scheinberg. Learning in these yeshivos our first two years of marriage clearly cemented for Dovid and I the kind of Torah lifestyle we wanted to lead in the future years, for ourselves and our children. As a young, newly married couple we were extremely fortunate to benefit from going to *shiurim* given frequently by R. Scheinberg for men and women (separately) and also having a private audience with the Rosh Yeshiva whenever we had a *she'elah*. We were always awed by his remarkable Torah knowledge and how he could "really sense what our problem was" and was able to skillfully guide us on any halachic or *shalom bayis* matter that came up in our marriage. When Dovid became ill, R. Scheinberg helped us out so many times with different *she'elos* that came up and his words of *chizuk* for us in our most distraught times helped us keep our *bitachon* strong in *HaKadosh Baruch Hu*. I am truly humbled by the beautiful *haskamah* that R. Scheinberg gave me for this book.

There is no question that the couple that my husband owed the most *hakaras ha-tov* to is Eugene and Doris Cohn. As a teenager, my husband lived with this couple for a few years. This act of *gemillas chasadim* truly had an unbelievable ripple effect for Dovid's entire family as the Cohns' quiet but sincere observance of Orthodox Judaism influenced my husband and his mother, sister, and brother to learn more about their Jewish roots and eventually all of them became religious. My children and I are still very much in touch with our "beloved Bubby and Zayde Cohn." May *HaKadosh Baruch Hu* bless them with many, many more happy and healthy years together.

My husband also often spoke about a Rav in the community of Memphis, Tennessee, Rav Nota Greenblatt, who he greatly admired and respected. Rav Nota was the person who originally made the connection between the Feldbaum family and the Cohns, and Dovid and his siblings were extremely grateful for how Rav Nota took such an interest in a family that he barely knew. Dovid was also extremely appreciative of how the Jewish community in Memphis sponsored my in-laws when they wanted to come to America after the war. I remember how my mother-in-law, with much warmth and affection, always praised this Jewish community for helping them start their new lives in America.

Two other couples who my husband was extremely close with in Israel and who are still very much in contact with me and my children are R. Dovid and Rena Krohn and Yisroel Chaim and Menucha Dudovitz. The Krohns are an extremely outgoing and warm couple. As Dovid's Rebbe, R. Krohn became very instrumental in encouraging his learning and yeshiva lifestyle by his own modest example. I have personally learned so much from Rena, in the way she raised such a fine family and the extreme comfortableness and warmth everyone feels when they step over the threshold of the Krohns' apartment. Dovid's closest friend in Eretz Yisrael was Yisroel Chaim, who married my good friend, Menucha. On the last day of the *Sheloshim* for Dovid, Yisroel Chaim and Menucha made a *bris* for their newborn son whom they named after my husband and Yisroel Chaim's grandfather, Dovid Zisman. There are no words that can truly express what a tremendous *nechamah* that was for me at that very, very difficult time.

I have always had an extremely close relationship with Dovid's family, Rita Feldbaum (a"h), Avraham and Dena Feldbaum, and R. Boruch and Nina (a"h) Rappaport. I miss my mother-in-law very much, an unbelievably talented woman who went along with her children's desire to become religious, made *aliyah* to live near them and spent her last years trying to have an influence on recent Russian immigrants to the country. My husband's siblings and their spouses offered us a constant source of support, strength, and *chizuk* during the crucial years when we were going through our *nisayon*. Though they all lived in Eretz Yisrael and were on a tight monetary budget, they did not hesitate to pick up the phone and stay in touch with us as often as possible. To this day, I am in close contact with all of them. It is particularly heartwarming to me that my niece (Avraham and Dena's daughter) and her husband, Nechama and Meir Kraut, have chosen to live in Baltimore for a few years and that they honored my husband by naming their firstborn child after him.

Unfortunately, there was a time of tragedy in the Feldbaum family where my mother-in-law, sister-in-law, and husband all passed away within two years of each other. Somehow all of the surviving children, spouses, and grandchildren bonded together to remain strong in the face of these incredible losses. My brother-in-law, Boruch, remarried a very special woman, Raizy, who was an *almanah* for many years, and they have created a beautiful *bayis ne'eman b'Yisrael* for their thirteen children, two of whom are from this second marriage. They are my personal example and inspiration of how life truly can go on happily after being faced with the heartbreaking losses of loving spouses.

I would also like to wish my father-in-law, Shmuel Feldbaum, many more happy years where he will continue to get much nachas from the Feldbaum/Rappaport families.

There is a famous saying, "Behind every great man there is a great woman." I want to re-phrase that quote a bit and say, "Behind every good writer there is a great editor!" My complete and total gratitude goes to Bracha Steinberg, my very special editor at Feldheim Publishers, who gave me the direction and insight on how this book should be written. After working with Bracha for over two years, I sincerely feel that I have grown leaps and bounds as a writer. Thank you, Bracha, for everything, but most of all, for believing in *me*.

A genuine *hakaras ha-tov* goes to R' Yaakov Feldheim, who originally met with me in Israel to see my skeletal outline for a book and decided to give my book idea a chance. I am so appreciative of R' Feldheim for letting me have the privilege of joining other authors worldwide who have had their books published by Feldheim Publishers. Thanks also go to members of the design, editorial, and production staff of Feldheim Publishers in Jerusalem for their professional work on my book, including: Mrs. Eden Chachamtzedek, typesetter, who was very attuned to any corrections or clarifications that needed to be made; Mr. Michael Silverstein, graphic artist, who did such a beautiful job designing the cover; Mrs. Joyce Bennett, Miss Penina Swift, Mrs. Deena Nataf, and R' Menachem Deutsch.

A month after I gave Feldheim Publishers a copy of my completed manuscript, the horrific terrorist attack on the Twin Towers in New York took place on September 11, 2001. This happened after months of homicide bombings in my beloved Eretz Yisrael, which, unfortunately, are still continuing to this day. After "9/11," I was literally not able to work on any rewrites for this book or submit my humorous magazine articles into the *Where, What and When* for months. I was "professionally paralyzed" and heartbroken at knowing how many more new *almanim, almanos,* and *yesomim* there were in *Klal Yisrael* and in the world. I sincerely hope that whoever reads this book will be able to offer those people who were so enormously affected by these cruel terrorist attacks the help that they may need. May God bless all of you and give you strength!

Rebecca Bram Feldbaum

Glossary

The following glossary provides a partial explanation of some of the Hebrew, Yiddish (Y.), and Aramaic (A.) words and phrases used in this book. The spellings and explanations reflect the way the specific word is used herein. Often, there are alternative spellings and meanings for the words.

A"H: acronym for *alav ha-shalom*, lit., "may peace be upon him"; may he rest in peace.

AGUNAH: a woman whose husband is missing or refuses to divorce his wife.

ALIYAH: lit., "ascent"; immigration to the Land of Israel; being called up to the reading of the Torah.

ALMANAH: a widow.

AVEILUS: mourning.

AVI HAYESOMIM: the Father of orphans (God).

BARUCH HASHEM: "Thank God!"; "Praise God!"

BAYIS NE'EMAN B'YISRAEL: an everlasting Jewish home.

BEN/BAS BAYIS: a guest who is treated as a member of the household.

BERACHAH: a blessing.

BIMAH: a raised platform in the synagogue for the Torah reading.

BRIS: the ritual of circumcision; the celebration of the occasion.

CHALLAH: a festive Sabbath loaf.

CHAMETZ: leavened foods, prohibited during Pesach.

CHAVRUSA: (A.) a Torah study partner.

CHESED: lovingkindness.

251

CHEVRAH: one's circle of friends.

CHIZUK: encouragement; strengthening of faith.

CHOL HA-MOED: the intermediate days of the Festivals of Sukkos and Pesach.

CHOLENT: a savory Sabbath stew kept warm overnight.

CHUMASH: [one of the] Five Books of Moses.

CHUPPAH: the wedding canopy; marriage.

DAVEN: (Y.) pray.

EREV SHABBOS: the day before Shabbos, that is, Friday.

EREV YOM KIPPUR: the day before Yom Kippur.

EREV YOM TOV: the day before a Festival.

GELT: (Y.) lit., "gold"; money.

GEMILLAS CHASADIM: acts of lovingkindness.

HAKADOSH BARUCH HU: the Holy One, Blessed is He (God).

HAKARAS HA-TOV: gratitude

HALACHAH: Jewish law.

HAMOTZI: "Who brings forth [bread from the earth]," the blessing recited over bread.

HANAVI: the Prophet.

HASKAMAH: approbation.

HAVDALAH: the blessings recited at the conclusion of Sabbaths and Festivals, separating the holy day from the other days of the week.

KASHER: to make something kosher.

KASHRUS: the Jewish dietary laws.

KIDDUSH: Sanctification of the Sabbath and Festivals, usually recited over a cup of wine.

KOS SHEL BERACHAH: a cup of wine over which a blessing was made.

KUGEL: (Y.) a baked vegetable or noodle pudding.

KVETCH: (Y.) to complain.

LEVAYAH: a funeral.

MECHITZAH: the partition that separates the men's and women's sections in a synagogue.

MEGILLAH: a scroll; the Scroll of Esther, read on Purim.

MENSCH: (Y.) lit., "a man"; a decent human being.

MIDDOS: [positive] character traits.

MINYAN: a quorum of at least ten adult males, necessary for con-
gregational prayer.

MI-SHEBERACH: "May He Who blessed...", the opening words of
the blessing for those called up to the Torah, including
prayers for the congregation, new mothers, and sick people.

NECHAMAH: consolation.

NISAYON: a trial; a challenge.

PARASHAH: the weekly Torah portion.

PETIRAH: death.

REFA'ENU: "Heal us," the opening words of the prayer for health
and healing contained in the daily prayer service.

RIBONO SHEL OLAM: Master of the Universe.

SECHACH: a covering of branches or straw mat used for the roof
of the *sukkah.*

SEFER BEREISHIS: the Book of Genesis.

SEUDAH: a festive meal.

SHACHARIS: the morning prayer service.

SHADCHAN: a matchmaker.

SHALACH MANOS: (Y.) gift packages of food sent on Purim.

SHALOM ALEICHEM: "Peace upon you," the opening words of
the traditional song addressed to the ministering angels on
Friday night before the Sabbath meal.

SHALOM BAYIS: domestic harmony.

SHE'ELAH: a halachic question.

SHEMONEH ESREI: lit., "eighteen"; the basic daily prayer service,
which originally contained eighteen blessings.

SHEVA BERACHOS: lit., "seven blessings"; blessings recited at a
wedding; the festive meals held for newlyweds during the
first week after their wedding, at the conclusion of which the
seven blessings are recited.

SHIDDUCH: a marital match.

SHIVAH: lit., "seven"; the seven days of mourning.

SHLEP: (Y.) to haul; to drag.

SHOFAR: a ram's horn, blown on Rosh Hashanah.

SHOMER SHABBOS: Sabbath-observant.

SHUL: (Y.) a synagogue.

SIDDUR: the prayer book.

SIMCHAH: joy; a joyous occasion.

SIYYATA DI'SHEMAYA: Divine assistance.

SUKKAH: a temporary hut in which Jews dwell during the Festival of Sukkos.

TATTI: (Y.) Daddy.

TEFILLIN: phylacteries; four Scriptural sections written on parchment, enclosed in black leather boxes and worn by men on the head and arm during morning prayers.

VORT: (Y.) lit., "a word"; a brief Torah discourse.

YAHRTZEIT: the anniversary of a death.

YASOM (YESOMIM): a person(s) who is orphaned of his mother or father.

ZECHUS: privilege; merit.

ZEMIROS: Sabbath hymns.